VA CLAIM SECRETS

VA CLAIM
SECRETS

**EXPERT TIPS AND PROVEN
STRATEGIES TO WIN YOUR
VA DISABILITY CLAIM FASTER**

BRIAN REESE

AUTHOR OF *YOU DESERVE IT*

HOUNDSTOOTH
PRESS

VA CLAIM SECRETS

Expert Tips and Proven Strategies to Win Your VA Disability Claim Faster

FIRST EDITION

ISBN 978-1-5445-4555-4 *Paperback*
978-1-5445-4554-7 *Ebook*

This book is dedicated to you. Us. Veterans. Here's to the brave ones who raised their right hands and took the oath to support and defend the Constitution of the United States against all enemies, foreign and domestic. For that, I salute you and stand alongside you forever.

CONTENTS

DISCLAIMER

THIS BOOK AND ALL ITS CONTENTS ARE PRESENTED SOLELY for informational and educational purposes. The author and publisher are not offering it as legal, financial, accounting, medical, or other professional services advice. While best efforts have been made in preparing this book, the author and publisher make no representations or warranties of any kind and assume no liabilities of any kind with respect to the accuracy or completeness of the contents. The author and publisher assume no responsibility for errors, inaccuracies, omissions, or any other inconsistencies herein.

Neither the author nor the publisher shall be held liable or responsible to any person or entity with respect to any loss or incidental or consequential damages caused, or alleged to have been caused, directly or indirectly, by the contents or programs contained herein. Every individual is different, and the knowledge, advice, and strategies contained herein may not be suitable for your situation. You should seek the services of a licensed and competent professional in your jurisdiction before beginning any program.

AUTHOR'S NOTE

THE BOOK YOU HOLD IN YOUR HANDS IS A COMPILATION OF my life's work. It is the culmination of ten-plus years and more than ten thousand hours teaching, training, and equipping veterans with VA disability-claim tips and strategies.

I have one goal for this book: to change your life. I hope you'll read it diligently, ponder the contents, apply the concepts that pertain to your situation, and receive every penny you deserve for serving our country.

From one veteran to another: thank you for your service and sacrifice. I appreciate you.

—BRIAN REESE, US AIR FORCE VETERAN, 2003–2012

INTRODUCTION

THE DAY I LEFT THE UNITED STATES AIR FORCE, WITH A variety of physical and mental ailments, was the first day I heard about the US Department of Veterans Affairs (VA). During my Transition Assistance Program, a representative from the VA in Boston gave a one-hour presentation that basically said, "If you have some stuff going on, you may be eligible for benefits," but it was already way too late for me. It was 2012, and I had multiple undiagnosed conditions from a combat deployment to Afghanistan. Even then, it would be several more years before I figured out that the physical and mental pains I suffered were service-related disabilities I could receive government compensation for.

According to our data, eight out of ten disabled veterans are *not* receiving the full benefits they deserve by law.[1] That means potentially more than 80 percent of you reading this

---

1   Statistics adapted from a survey performed by VA Claims Insider of more than one thousand veterans with disability ratings; 87 percent of respondents reported that their ratings did not represent their disabilities.

now are missing out on available money you earned for serving our country. And that's if you have a VA disability rating at all. Of the roughly 18 million veterans alive today, only about 5.6 million, or 31 percent (yep, around one in four veterans), receive *any* VA disability benefits at all.[2] That means around 70 percent of veterans alive today get nothing! That's shameful to me, and I'm on a mission to change it.

How is all of this possible? First, there's a lack of awareness due in part to inadequate education. That was my problem.

Second, the system Congress created, which the VA has to operate in, is complicated and confusing. There are so many addenda and amendments to eligibility rules that many of you may have given up on applying.

Some of you may have jumped through all the hoops to successfully apply but received a denial or an "underrating" (meaning the VA acknowledged some kind of disability but disagreed about its origin or severity). If that's you, you are understandably *frustrated*. You probably spent dozens of hours searching online, combing the VA.gov website, collecting the documents you needed, and attempting to navigate the system only to feel unseen or, worse, like you've been called a liar.

You're not a liar. The problem isn't you. Nor is it the VA, honestly! The VA is not trying to keep money from you. It wants to help you. *The problem is the system.* That's where I come in.

You served. You deserve.

---

2   Jonathan E. Vespa, "Those Who Served: America's Veterans from World War II to the War on Terror," United States Census Bureau, June, 2020, https://www.census.gov/content/dam/Census/library/publications/2020/demo/acs-43.pdf; Veterans Benefits Administration, Annual Benefits Report: Fiscal Year 2023 (Washington, DC: U.S. Department of Veterans Affairs, 2024), 73, https://www.benefits.va.gov/REPORTS/abr/docs/2023-abr.pdf.

MY PATH TO PURPOSE

Generally speaking, I was lucky. I was put in touch with a veteran service organization called American Veterans (AMVETS), and a skilled officer helped me navigate the disability application process. I was able to get a VA disability rating for my service-connected disabilities. But it would be another six years before I got the full benefits I deserved. I didn't even know you could be underrated! There was no comprehensive resource to help me educate myself on the topic.

Over those six years, I lost almost $100,000 in tax-free benefits I deserved by law. I lost that money simply because I didn't know any better.

Meanwhile, even with my VA rating, I wasn't getting the mental health care I needed because I wasn't being fully honest with myself. I eventually hit rock bottom, too broken to stand on my own two feet. And then, through prayer and being open and vulnerable, I finally got help.

Part of that help came from a coach who forced me to answer really tough questions about who I am and what my purpose is. I realized that God put me on Earth to serve fellow veterans and give them *hope*. To show them there can be beauty in the brokenness.

Then I thought, *Well, I know a lot about the VA disability system. Most veterans know very little about it, yet we all desperately need to understand it.* So, I started VA Claims Insider, which is now the largest community of veterans helping veterans worldwide. At VA Claims Insider, we use what we call the SEM (Strategy, Education, Medical Evidence) Method to help veterans like you get the VA disability compensation they deserve as quickly as possible.

When you wear the uniform, you're connected with other service members whose situations are similar to yours in meaningful ways. Then, you take the uniform off and are surrounded by people who can't possibly comprehend what you've experienced. You feel separated from the reality everybody else lives in. I hear stories like this all the time.

People come to VA Claims Insider not only for help with financial benefits but because they crave identity, community, and purpose. They want to feel important again. Our fellow veterans tell us they feel lost after service. They feel like people hear the word "veteran" and immediately think they're broken or crazy. This leads them to pretend everything's fine and ignore whatever struggles they face.

But you might not be fine—and that's okay. It's okay to not be okay! You experienced tough stuff while you served, and now, you're processing it. This is exactly why there are resources to help you. The VA exists to help you. And my company, VA Claims Insider, exists to make sure you get that help.

Being in a community with other veterans has been hugely therapeutic for me. I got my identity and my life back, and I want to help you do the same.

NEED IMMEDIATE HELP?

I will cover mental health resources in depth later, but if you are thinking about taking your own life, call 988 and press 1, or chat with someone online at VeteransCrisisLine.net. America loses roughly seventeen veterans to suicide every day.[3] Please don't be one of them.

---

3   George Petras, "Veteran Suicide Rate Is Down, but Nearly 17 Soldiers Take Their Own Lives Every Day," *USA Today*, September 21, 2023, https://www.usatoday.com/story/graphics/2023/09/21/veteran-suicide-rate-2023-decreases/70909134007/.

WHAT YOU WILL LEARN IN THIS BOOK

From these pages, you will learn how to get the VA disability rating and compensation you deserve by law. In fact, if you apply the strategies in this book, you will probably walk away with hundreds of thousands of dollars.

This book is not a series of tricks to help you file false claims or get what you don't deserve. That's wrong and illegal. This book is a blueprint—a clear, straightforward, no-nonsense, checklist-style guide—to help you legally obtain the benefits you earned during your service.

However, this book is definitely not exhaustive. There's so much information out there that trying to tell you everything would only confuse you and hamstring your motivation. If there's one thing I want to do, it is to motivate you. So, I've kept this to what I believe are the most critical items you need to know. This is your action plan to get what is owed to you.

The sole purpose of this book is to educate and inspire veterans to take action. Only through action can you finally get the federal and state benefits you deserve by law.

I can't emphasize the word "action" enough. If you simply read this book as a passive observer and don't act on its contents, you will not get anything. Think about this brilliant quote by George Bernard Shaw: "...if you teach a man anything he will never learn it..."[4]

Knowledge is not power. Knowledge is knowledge, and power is power. But knowledge can become power through action. And this is your action moment!

You can start taking action by getting the most out of this book. Here are seven tips:

---

4   George Bernard Shaw, *Back to Methuselah: A Metabiological Pentateuch* (New York: Brentano's, 1921), xiii.

1. Before you skip a section completely, stop to ask, "How does this concept fit into the bigger picture?" Although there may be sections of this book that don't pertain to your specific needs, most of the content is intertwined, and each section builds on the last.

2. Highlight, underline, and crease the most important pages of this book. Some of the content is complicated, although I've done my best to keep it simple. Mark the parts you know you'll need to find again later.

3. Look for ways to teach these concepts to other veterans. The best way to master a concept is to teach it. And what a great way to serve other veterans in the process!

4. Set a clear goal for when you will finally get the benefits you deserve and mark it on the calendar. Will it happen exactly on that timeline? Maybe, maybe not. But if you don't set a goal, you may never do it at all. Hold yourself accountable for your own results. Nobody should care more about your benefits than you do.

5. Don't be afraid to fail! There are so many factors involved in the rating process that even if you do everything "right," you still might not get the rating you deserve the first time around. It'll feel like a gut punch. That's when you get back up off the ground and punch back. The VA disability process never ends. Unless you quit. But we won't let you quit.

6. Keep a journal of the most important concepts in this book that apply to you. Writing forces clear thinking. In the process, you'll create a personalized tip sheet of helpful strategies and lessons learned.

7. Stay up to date, and educate yourself! Laws and rules change often. The concepts in this book are evergreen, but some of the specifics may change. Scan the QR codes throughout this book for direct links to expert-level educational

resources. The bonus resources at the end of this book list some websites where you can find great information.

Yes, I said that this book will make the process of getting your benefits as simple as possible—but simple is not always easy. When things get hard, I'm here to help you get back up, get into the ring, and throw a few more punches. I will never let you quit nor will I let you fail.

That's why I've written this book: to provide the education, strategy, and resources you need to qualify for VA disability benefits worth hundreds of thousands of dollars. Maybe even millions of dollars.

Would that change your life? I think so.

Take a moment to sit still, close your eyes, and breathe. Imagine having more tax-free compensation for you and your family. Imagine being able to give more back to society. Imagine going to the doctor and being uncomfortably vulnerable about your disability conditions and getting the help and treatment you need.

You *can* have all these things and more, but you must will them into existence through your actions! Nobody is going to do this for you. We will lead you through the labyrinth that is VA disability claims, but you must be the one to conquer it.

Herbert Spencer once remarked, "For the great aim of education is not knowledge, but action."[5] Fellow veterans, this is an action book.

LFG!!!

---

5   Dale Carnegie, *How to Win Friends and Influence People* (New York: Simon and Schuster, 1936).

PART I

EDUCATION

CHAPTER 1

★ ★ ★

THE PURPOSE OF THE VA

FOR A LONG TIME, AS A FORMER OFFICER IN THE US AIR Force, I believed it wasn't possible for me to have a mental health condition. *I'm too strong*, I thought. *I need to take care of our troops and their well-being.* I didn't realize I couldn't take care of anybody else unless I took care of myself first.

I coped by turning to alcohol and drugs, but I became addicted, and that led to all kinds of destruction. My marriage ended in divorce. I struggled at work and eventually resigned. I lost most of my friendships. I pushed loved ones away. At the time, I thought I was the only veteran suffering from a mental health condition—which, in retrospect, is bonkers, but that's how it felt. So, I suffered alone and in silence.

But that's the whole purpose of the VA: to take care of veterans. Those who served deserve. I'm going to keep reminding you of that throughout our journey together.

THE HISTORY OF THE VA

The idea behind the VA goes back to the earliest days of our nation. The first American statute designed to care for veterans was a Plymouth Colony law enacted in 1636 that provided pensions for soldiers wounded in battle. Then, shortly after the start of the Revolutionary War, to encourage enlistments and reduce desertions, the fledgling nation promised financial aid to any soldier or sailor injured in the service of the colonies who couldn't earn a living as a result. Later, during the Civil War, the General Pension Act expanded the idea by providing payments to Union soldiers based on their degree of disability.

Over the next fifty years, even as progress led to the development of better care for veterans and their families, federal veterans' programs still lacked a unified governing body to oversee and standardize operations. The first comprehensive consolidation effort of federal veterans' programs wouldn't happen until after World War I, when Congress created the Veterans Bureau, which Herbert Hoover later made into a federal administration and renamed the Veterans Administration. The VA finally became a cabinet-level executive department under Ronald Reagan. George H. W. Bush hailed the new department at the time of its official creation, saying, "There is only one place for the Veterans of America, in the Cabinet Room, at the table with the President of the United States of America."[6]

Today's VA is responsible for serving the needs of those injured in our nation's defense and the families of those injured or killed in service by providing healthcare, disability compensation and rehabilitation, education assistance, home loans, and national cemetery services, among other services and benefits.

---

6   "VA History," US Department of Veterans Affairs, last updated March 6, 2024, https://department.
    va.gov/history/history-overview/.

The VA is the largest healthcare system in the world! It's also the largest provider and supporter of telehealth services in the world. As we stand in the present and look toward the future, the very existence of the VA helps us remember our storied past, all who have served or are serving, and all who honor America's veterans.

TWENTY VA CLAIMS MYTHS DEBUNKED

The primary purpose of VA disability compensation is to make up for the potential economic loss of civilian wages or working time due to or for tending to (appointments, etc.) your service-connected disability conditions. It's essentially the US government saying, "Thanks for your service. You sacrificed much for America, including your health and well-being. We accept that your reduced health may impact your ability to live and provide for your family as compared to if you had not been injured."

However, too often veterans don't apply for benefits because of myths surrounding their administration. So, let me set the record straight once and for all.

Myth #1: "VA disability is only for those veterans who are more 'disabled' than I am. Other veterans deserve benefits but not me."

Fact: Almost all veterans are eligible for VA disability benefits, except those with a dishonorable discharge that hasn't been upgraded. If you have any kind of disability as a result of your honorable service, then, guess what? You deserve benefits.

Myth #2: "If I get VA disability benefits, it will take away from another veteran's benefits."

Fact: Your VA disability benefits do not affect any other veteran's benefits. They are completely independent of one another. If you choose not to get your benefits, the only people you're hurting are yourself and your family.

Myth #3: "I've been out of the service too long to apply for VA disability benefits."

Fact: There is no statute of limitations on VA disability benefits. You can apply for benefits at any time. There are no restrictions.

Myth #4: "My conditions weren't documented in my military medical records, so I'll just get denied."

Fact: You don't need your condition(s) recorded in your Service Treatment Records (STRs) nor do you need to have been diagnosed during service. But your conditions do need to be diagnosed and documented in a medical record, such as VA or private medical records. If you think you have a disability but haven't yet been diagnosed, please consider going to see a doctor or other healthcare professional.

Myth #5: "The VA already gave me a VA disability rating, so I can't apply again."

Fact: The VA disability process is never over unless you quit. You can apply as many times as you'd like. Maybe your conditions have worsened, so you want to file for an increase. Perhaps you realize you're eligible for secondary service connection and want to file a secondary claim. DO IT! Just make sure you have medical evidence to back up your assertions.

Myth #6: "My Veteran Service Officer (VSO) said I should be happy with my VA disability rating percentage and not rock the boat."

Fact: The only time you should be happy with your VA disability rating percentage is if you believe you're getting everything you're legally, morally, ethically, and medically eligible for. If you think you deserve an increase, open a new claim on the VA.gov website and file for it!

Myth #7: "I already got denied before, so there's nothing else I can do about it. If I apply again, the VA will just deny me again."

Fact: Previous denials don't necessarily impact future claims. There are plenty of options if the VA previously denied your claim. You can file a Higher Level Review (HLR) or a supplemental claim. If those get denied, you can file a records-only Board Appeal or request a video teleconference with a Board of Veterans' Appeals (BVA) judge. There is always another path, but you must stay in the process and never quit!

Myth #8: "If I apply for a VA rating increase, the VA will reduce my current rating."

Fact: This is highly unlikely. The VA generally only reviews the specific disability condition(s) in your current application and nothing else.

Myth #9: "The VA has it out for veterans and intentionally denies their disability claims."

Fact: The VA does not intentionally deny claims. They're following laws and regulations when reviewing your VA disability claim. Help them help you by submitting a strong claim with the appropriate medical evidence!

Myth #10: "My disabilities aren't severe enough to get a VA rating."

Fact: Regardless of the severity of your symptoms, you can still get your condition connected to your service, even if it's at the minimum rating of 0 percent (noncompensable). This is important because if your condition worsens over time, it's easier to file for an increase on a disability that's already been deemed to be service connected.

Myth #11: "If I get seen for mental health conditions or have a VA rating for PTSD, the VA will take away my guns."

Fact: Your VA rating for mental health conditions, including PTSD, has nothing to do with your guns. By law, the VA can't take away your guns. It would be an unlawful seizure without a warrant. However, even though the VA does not have the authority to take away your guns or impose any other limitations based on ratings, VA ratings can potentially impact other aspects of a veteran's life, and I encourage you to consider your own individual circumstances.

Myth #12: "If I get a VA rating for mental health conditions or have a VA rating for PTSD, I'll lose my security clearance."

Fact: Your VA rating for mental health conditions, including PTSD, has nothing to do with your security clearance. If you do have a mental health condition and are seeking treatment and taking medications, you need to notify your program security official to update your SF-86. However, doing so won't impact your security clearance. Please note that although a rating alone may not impact a security clearance, failure to disclose it may be considered a lack of integrity and honesty and can impact a security clearance.

Myth #13: "My VA rating for mental health should be higher because I was a [insert your MOS here]."

Fact: Your VA rating for mental health has nothing to do with your job in the military. It has everything to do with the current frequency, severity, and duration of your symptoms and your individual circumstances.

Myth #14: "If I get a VA disability rating (physical condition or mental health), my employer will find out and take negative action against me."

Fact: Your employer has no way of knowing this information unless you tell them. If an employer takes negative action against you because of your VA disability, it could be a violation of the Americans with Disabilities Act (ADA).

Myth #15: "If I get a 100 percent VA rating or permanent and total disability (P&T) status, I can't work anymore."

Fact: Your VA disability rating percentage does not impact your ability to work. Income and VA disability benefits are independent of each other. The only time work status can be affected is if you're rated 100 percent Total Disability Individual Unemployability (TDIU). If you have TDIU, you can only earn up to the federal poverty limit for that year without affecting your TDIU status.

Myth #16: "Once my conditions are service connected, I must go to the VA for all my medical care and treatment."

Fact: You do not need to go to the VA for medical care unless you want to. Many veterans have private insurance and choose to see private doctors in their local area.

Myth #17: "I should have a VA rating because the VA medically diagnosed me and is treating me for the condition."

Fact: Just because you receive medical care at the VA for a specific condition does not mean that condition is eligible for VA benefits under the law. All disabilities must be "service connected," meaning they were caused or made worse by your military service or another service-connected disability.

Myth #18: "If I go to 90 percent or 100 percent, the VA will schedule me for a reexamination of all of my service-connected disabilities."

Fact: Getting a 90 percent or 100 percent VA disability does not affect other disability conditions. The VA generally only reviews conditions when they are not static and have been scheduled for a routine future examination or when a new claim is filed for a specific disability condition(s) that was the subject of a previous file. Think of this as well: the VA doesn't have the time to go back and review everything!

Myth #19: "There aren't any additional benefits for my dependents if I get 100 percent P&T status."

Fact: There are tons of additional benefits available to the dependents of veterans with a 100 percent P&T rating. Check out our website at VAClaimsInsider.com for a complete list of benefits.

Myth #20: "Accredited VSOs and claims agents offer the same services as VA Claims Insider except the accredited system works for free."

Fact: Accredited VSOs and claims agents represent veterans with power of attorney (POA) before the VA. They prepare and file your VA claim for you, interact with the VA, and act on your behalf. In contrast, VA Claims Insider is an education company, not a VSO, claims agent, or law firm. We are a dedicated team of fellow veterans and veteran advocates; we are not accredited. Our primary focuses are VA disability education—both live and on demand—and helping fulfill medical evidence requirements (Disability Benefits Questionnaires [DBQs], Nexus Letters, and Mental Health Independent Medical Opinions) through our preferred provider network. These two service areas allow us to help eligible veterans increase their VA rating, win previously denied VA disability benefits, and uncover high-value secondary VA disabilities based on medical evidence of record. VA Claims Insider does not assist veterans with the preparation, presentation, and prosecution of VA disability claims for VA benefits. Accredited claims agents and attorneys can charge up to 33 1/3 percent of your back pay as their fee for helping with your claim. If you look at a claim that takes thirty-six months to win on appeal in 2024 and you go from an overall rating of 30 percent to 70 percent, an accredited claims agent or attorney could charge you more than $14,160.

Remember, the Department of Veterans Affairs exists to take

care of veterans who served. If you served, you're a veteran. The VA exists both for you and because of you! And if you are eligible for disability compensation—a tax-free monetary benefit that can be paid to you every month for the rest of your life—you deserve it.

ELIGIBILITY FOR VA DISABILITY COMPENSATION

But how do you know if you are even eligible for disability compensation? 38 U.S.C. § 101 defines a military veteran as: (1) a person who served in the active military, naval, air, or space service, and (2) who was discharged or released therefrom under conditions other than dishonorable.

The types of qualifying service listed under 38 CFR 3.6 include, but are not limited to:

- Active Duty Service
- Active Duty for Training (ADT), when a claim for service connection is based on a disability or death resulting from a disease or injury incurred or aggravated in the line of duty during any period of active duty for training
- Inactive Duty for Training (IADT), when a claim for service connection is based on disability or death resulting from an injury incurred or aggravated in the line of duty during any period of inactive duty training or myocardial infarction, cardiac arrest, or a cerebrovascular accident which occurred during such training

Assuming you meet these basic requirements, your VA benefits eligibility largely depends on your "Veteran Status" as determined by your DD214—i.e., character of service, length of service, service commitment, and the number of days spent on active-duty orders. This is especially important for National Guard and Reserve VA benefits.

In addition, at least one of these must be true:

- You got sick or injured while serving in the military and can link this condition to your illness or injury (called an "in-service disability"), or
- You had an illness or injury before you joined the military and serving made it worse (called a "pre-existing disability"), or
- You have a disability related to your active-duty service that didn't appear until after you ended your service (called a "post-service disability"), or
- You have a disability caused by or aggravated by an already service-connected disability (called a "secondary disability" for secondary service connection)

In later chapters, we will discuss how you can prove you meet these requirements, but first, let's discuss potential bars to eligibility.

CHARACTER OF DISCHARGE

The VA Character of Discharge determination, often referred to as a "Character of Service" determination, is a process used by the VA to assess the nature of a veteran's discharge from the military. The Character of Discharge can significantly affect a veteran's entitlement to certain VA benefits and compensation.

Military discharges can vary widely, but they are typically categorized into five main types:

- Honorable Discharge: Typically allows veterans to access the full range of VA benefits

- General Discharge: May or may not allow access to certain VA benefits depending on the specific circumstances and any underlying misconduct
- Other Than Honorable (OTH) Discharge: Often results in limited access to VA benefits, and certain benefits, such as the GI Bill, may be restricted or denied
- Bad Conduct Discharge (BCD): Usually leads to a loss of most VA benefits, but some medical and mental health services may still be available.
- Dishonorable Discharge: Generally results in a loss of all VA benefits and services.

Veterans who receive less than an Honorable Discharge may have the option to seek a discharge upgrade through a military Discharge Review Board (DRB) or a Board for Correction of Military Records (BCMR). This is known as a VA Character of Discharge review, and a successful upgrade can improve the veteran's VA benefits eligibility.

WILLFUL MISCONDUCT

Willful misconduct—or deliberate wrongdoing with knowledge of or wanton and reckless disregard of its probable consequences—can also bar you from VA benefits eligibility. Examples of willful misconduct include:

- Alcohol and Drug Abuse: Willful misconduct often comes into play when a veteran's disability or condition is a direct result of excessive alcohol or drug use. This can include injuries or health conditions arising from alcohol-related accidents, drug overdoses, or other substance-abuse-related incidents.

- Criminal Activity: Engaging in criminal activities that result in injuries or harm to oneself or others can be considered willful misconduct. This may include incidents such as fights, altercations, or illegal drug transactions.
- Self-inflicted Injuries: Deliberate acts of self-harm or suicide attempts can also be categorized as willful misconduct.

According to 38 CFR 3.301(a), the VA may award direct service connection only when a disability or cause of death was incurred or aggravated in the line of duty—but not when it was the result of the veteran's own willful misconduct.

LINE OF DUTY DETERMINATION

A Line of Duty (LOD) determination is a process used by the military to determine the circumstances under which an injury, illness, or death occurred while an individual was performing their official duties. The purpose of an LOD determination is to establish whether the incident or condition is duty related, which can have significant implications for benefits, compensation, and administrative actions.

Types of LODs:

- Line of Duty (LOD): If the incident or condition is found to be in the line of duty, the individual is typically entitled to benefits and compensation, including medical care and disability benefits, if the injury or illness is service connected.
- Not in the Line of Duty (NLOD): If the incident or condition is determined not to be in the line of duty, the individual may not be eligible for certain benefits or may face administrative actions, depending on the circumstances.

When making an LOD determination, several factors are considered, including the circumstances surrounding the incident, whether the individual was on official duty, whether misconduct or negligence was involved, and whether the injury or illness is service connected. The process can vary depending on the specific agency and its regulations, but it typically involves an investigation, interviews, and the gathering of evidence to make an informed decision.

If an individual disagrees with the LOD determination, they may have the right to appeal the decision through a formal process within their respective agency or organization.

In the next chapter, I'll tell you everything you need to know about the disability claims process, from getting quality help to proving your disability is service related. With comprehensive education, you can create an effective application strategy. Then you can file a strong and verifiable claim that gets you the compensation you deserve!

CHAPTER 2

★ ★ ★

THE DISABILITY CLAIMS PROCESS

ALTHOUGH THE VA DISABILITY CLAIMS PROCESS CAN SEEM daunting, it doesn't have to be. It's all about educating yourself and simplifying the process into its most important parts, which I'll attempt to do in this chapter.

If (1) you suffer from any of the 834-plus disability conditions recognized by the VA, (2) your active-duty service caused those disability conditions or made them worse or a service-connected disability caused or aggravates your current disability condition, and (3) your disability conditions are limiting or affecting your work or life in a negative way, then, boom, you're eligible for benefits! But, of course, that's not the end of the story. You must prove it all.

This foundational chapter is the longest of the book, so bear with me. I'm going to explain all the basics so you can start a winning claim.

THREE ELEMENTS OF AN EFFECTIVE APPLICATION

Asking the VA to prove you are eligible for benefits is a recipe for disaster. They don't have the time! It's much better to advocate for yourself or work with an accredited representative. Either way, you can use the Caluza Triangle to understand the three elements of an effective application.

The Caluza Triangle came from a US Court of Appeals for Veterans Claims (Court) case called *Caluza v. Brown*. This case established a three-part test that a veteran must pass to get VA disability benefits:

1. Does the veteran have a medical diagnosis of a disability condition in a medical record?
2. Does the veteran have evidence of an in-service event, injury, disease, or aggravation?
3. Does the veteran establish a nexus (link between #1 and #2) via competent medical evidence?

If the answer to all three questions is "YES," a veteran's disability is considered service connected.

When the VA denies disability compensation claims, it's almost always because there isn't enough proof. In Part II, we will discuss exactly how to make your case on an "at least as likely as not" basis, but first, you'll need to understand each of these three elements.

MEDICAL DIAGNOSIS

The number-one thing you can do to improve the chances of a VA disability compensation claim approval is to have your condition(s) diagnosed and documented in a military, VA, or private medical record.

Say, for example, you're tired all the time, you wake up gasping for air, and you snore loudly, so you think you might have sleep apnea. A recent study found that 69 percent of Iraq and Afghanistan veterans had a high risk for sleep apnea and that this risk increased in those who also suffered from PTSD.[7] So, you're probably right—and eligible for benefits. But you won't get them just by telling the VA, "Hey, I've got sleep apnea, and it's due to my military service, so you connect the dots." Only a sleep study can confirm the presence of sleep apnea. Furthermore, if you weren't diagnosed on active duty, chances are you'll have a tough time connecting your sleep apnea directly to service (more on that in a bit).

In an ideal world, you wouldn't have to see a VA or private doctor now to get a diagnosis because you saw a military doctor while you were active. Therefore, your condition was diagnosed—and documented—during service. If your diagnosis came from a military doctor while you were in service, your claim will almost certainly be approved (as long as you can also prove that the condition is negatively affecting your work or livelihood and it is generally a chronic disability).

Unfortunately, many veterans never went to the doctor while they were in the military. Maybe they didn't want to seem or feel vulnerable. Maybe, in their unit, being sick carried a stigma. Maybe they didn't realize they had a medical condition. Or maybe they were just lazy. Whatever the reason, they don't have a record of their condition.

Fortunately, it's never too late to get your butt to a doctor. My humble advice is not to even try applying for VA disability

---

7   Peter J. Colvonen, et al., "Obstructive Sleep Apnea and Posttraumatic Stress Disorder among OEF/OIF/OND Veterans," *Journal of Clinical Sleep Medicine* 11, no. 5 (April 2015): 513–518, https://doi.org/10.5664/jcsm.4692.

compensation benefits until you've had that appointment. After all, you don't have any evidence of your condition until it's been diagnosed and documented in a medical record.

Even if your disability is documented in your STRs, it's helpful to get a current medical examination, opinion, and/ or diagnosis. Doing so establishes that you are still suffering severely from the symptoms of an illness, injury, exposure, or aggravation that occurred during your service or secondary to a service-connected disability.

EVIDENCE

To receive VA disability compensation, you must prove not only that you have a medical diagnosis, but you must also provide evidence that you experienced an in-service injury, disease, or aggravation or that your current service-connected disability caused or aggravated the claimed condition.

For example, Mary is a veteran who developed asthma while flying above Lebanon after September 11, 2001. Because Afghanistan, Djibouti, Egypt, Jordan, Lebanon, Syria, Uzbekistan, and Yemen—and the airspace above them—during this time period are listed under the PACT Act, there is sufficient evidence she was exposed to damaging airborne particulates. This is a "presumptive service connection," which we will discuss more later in this chapter.

In most cases, though, it's not enough to show that you experienced an injury or disease while in service nor that you have a current diagnosis. You must also connect the event to the condition.

NEXUS

When you make an argument that your disability is connected to your service, the VA calls this connection a "nexus." Essentially, a nexus is a logical link between Event A and Condition B.

Ideally, your benefits application will include a thorough and factual Nexus Letter, which is an evidence-based document (advisory-type opinion) prepared by a private medical professional that helps establish a connection between the veteran's current disability and their active-duty military service. But not all Nexus Letters are created equally.

The strongest Nexus Letters include a statement with the words "more likely than not" or, at a minimum, "at least as likely as not." They also include all records reviewed and relevant medical research reports. Together, these elements give the Nexus Letter high probative value, meaning it reaches a high level of proof.

Speaking of probative value, let's discuss how the VA determines if your medical evidence is credible.

CREDIBILITY OF MEDICAL EVIDENCE

In my experience, most veterans don't have enough medical evidence to support their full VA disability claim. But even when they do, it is not always credible.

"Credibility" is a blanket term referring to whether evidence is believable or not believable. For example, if a veteran claims he injured his lower back in the air force while loading cargo onto a C-130 aircraft during an exercise in July 2002, and personnel records reflect his statement, then it is deemed credible. In contrast, if a veteran claims he injured his lower back during multiple parachute jumps in the army from 1980 through 1983, but personnel records show he was a clerk, his statement is not credible.

In addition, evidence must have probative value. In other words, it should:

- make a matter material to the determination more or less likely, and
- have sufficient weight, either by itself or in combination with other evidence, to persuade the decision-maker about a fact.

A veteran's STRs, for example, are generally highly probative, but they don't necessarily prove a service connection. A nexus between your current disability and an injury or disease you experienced during your service will be required to award service connection. That's why it's so important to get competent medical evidence from a current physician, or at least competent lay evidence.

"Competent medical evidence" means evidence provided by a person who is qualified through education, training, or experience to offer medical diagnoses, statements, or opinions. It also means the evidence contains statements conveying sound medical principles found in medical treatises and authoritative writings, such as medical and scientific articles and research reports or analyses.

"Competent lay evidence" means any evidence provided by someone not required to have specialized education, training, or experience. Lay evidence is competent if it is provided by a person who has knowledge of facts or circumstances surrounding your case and conveys matters that can be observed and described by a layperson.

The VA is required to accept medical and lay evidence from non-VA sources (e.g., private medical evidence) at face value unless there is reason to question its competency or credibility. In other words, non-VA evidence does not have inherently less probative value than evidence originated by the VA. The VA uses the following to determine the probative value of your evidence:

- competency
- credibility
- thoroughness
- precision
- relevancy
- date of the evidence

Below are examples of questions VA claims adjudicators consider when weighing medical evidence:

- Did the evidence originate in service or in close proximity to service?
- Is the medical opinion supported by clinical data and review of medical records?
- How detailed, clear, or persuasive is the opinion?
- Is the opinion based on personal knowledge or on history provided by another person?

It's important to note that the VA does not apply the "treating physician rule," which gives more weight to evidence from a treating physician than evaluations made by consulting physicians or expert witnesses. However, a treating physician's familiarity with the history of a disability may increase the probative value of any medical evidence/opinion.

It's also worth noting that when evaluating evidence, VA decision-makers must:

- be objective and fair in the consideration of evidence
- ensure that any inferences, findings, and conclusions made are supported under the facts and law
- follow the evidentiary guidance in M21-1
- be professional and courteous even when claimants are antagonistic, critical, or abusive
- not allow any bias or personal feelings into the evaluation of evidence or the decision
- not arbitrarily or capriciously refuse to assign weight to a claimant's evidence
- not adopt or express an adversarial position toward a claimant or beneficiary

Remember, the VA disability system is nonadversarial. There is no advocate on behalf of the VA opposing claims and no policy to minimize or deny benefits. VA decision-makers are expected to liberally apply VA's pro-veteran policies, procedures, and regulations to help you get the benefits you deserve.

So, let's talk now about the types of service connection you can claim in your Nexus Letter.

FIVE TYPES OF SERVICE CONNECTION

As we discussed, establishing a service connection for your disability—a nexus—is a crucial part of the disability claims process. But it's not always as simple as connecting your combat PTSD to the constant rocket and mortar attacks you experienced in Afghanistan. There are five different types of service connection you should understand so you can craft the best strategy for your application.

DIRECT SERVICE CONNECTION

Having a direct service connection means your current disability is the direct result of your active-duty military service. Perhaps it was a training incident, car accident, combat deployment, stress from the job, or any other in-service incident, injury, event, or disease that directly caused or aggravated your current disability.

Direct service connection may be established under 38 CFR 3.303(a) when (1) the evidence or a medical opinion shows a nexus between a current disability and an injury, disease, or event in service, or (2) competent medical evidence demonstrates continuous symptoms that are sufficient to constitute a nexus between a current disability and an injury, disease, or event in service. We will discuss what constitutes "competent medical evidence" later, but for now, understand that "continuous symptoms" refers to symptoms that continue without stopping or recur regularly with minimal interruptions.

If the medical evidence shows only isolated instances of symptoms, an examination with medical opinion, requested in accordance with 38 CFR 3.159(c)(4), may provide the required nexus. In other words, you may still be able to establish a direct service connection for your disability even if you have not had continuous symptoms since your service.

Here's a list of the ten most common VA claims:

1. Tinnitus
2. Limitation of Flexion, Knee
3. Hearing Loss
4. Post-Traumatic Stress Disorder (PTSD)
5. Lumbosacral or Cervical Strain
6. Paralysis of the Sciatic Nerve (Sciatica)
7. Scars, General

8. Limitation of Motion of the Ankle
9. Limitation of Motion of the Arm
10. Migraines

Here's a list of the ten easiest VA claims to prove:

1. Tinnitus
2. Mental Health Conditions
3. Headaches
4. Musculoskeletal Conditions
5. Gastroesophageal Reflux Disease (GERD) and Irritable Bowel Syndrome (IBS)
6. Radiculopathy
7. Obstructive Sleep Apnea (OSA)
8. Flat Feet and Plantar Fasciitis
9. Presumptive Conditions
10. Erectile Dysfunction (ED)

You can also see a list of the top one hundred VA disability claims when you scan the QR code below.

The following are the evidence requirements for a direct service connection:

- REQUIRED: DD214
- REQUIRED: Diagnosis of a current disability in a medi-

cal record (STRs, VA medical records, or private medical records)

- REQUIRED: Evidence of an in-service event, injury, disease, or aggravation in either STRs or military personnel records
- RECOMMENDED: Nexus Letter for Direct Service Connection (if you've been out of the military for more than twelve months and you either don't have clear evidence in your STRs or your claim was previously denied)
- OPTIONAL: Statement in Support of Claim (if you're trying to prove an in-service stressor event and it's not already documented in your STRs)
- OPTIONAL: Buddy Letter (if you're trying to prove an in-service stressor event and it's not already documented in your STRs)

SECONDARY SERVICE CONNECTION

In accordance with 38 CFR § 3.310, a secondary service connection means that your disability was caused or made worse by a different service-connected disability.

Let's say, for example, you contracted tinnitus while serving. Today, even though you are no longer serving, that service-connected tinnitus might be causing or aggravating your migraine headaches, anxiety, and/or depression. So, you could file a VA disability claim for migraine headaches secondary to your service-connected tinnitus.

The ten easiest secondary conditions to claim are:

1. Bruxism Secondary to Mental Health Conditions
2. Cause and Effect Secondary Musculoskeletal Conditions
3. ED Secondary to Mental Health Conditions
4. GERD Secondary to Mental Health Conditions

5. GERD Secondary to an Orthopedic Condition or Migraines Due to Use of NSAIDS
6. IBS Secondary to Mental Health Conditions and Use of NSAIDS
7. Mental Health Conditions Secondary to Any Service-Connected Disabilities or Physical Pain
8. Migraines Secondary to Mental Health Conditions and/or Tinnitus
9. Sleep Apnea Secondary to Sinusitis, Rhinitis, Deviated Septum, or Asthma
10. Vertigo Secondary to Mental Health Conditions and/or Tinnitus

To see the hundred-plus most common secondary conditions for VA disability claims, scan the QR code below to download my free ebook.

The following are the evidence requirements for a secondary service connection:

- REQUIRED: DD214
- REQUIRED: Diagnosis of a current secondary VA disability you're attempting to link to a current service-connected disability (must be documented in a medical record)
- REQUIRED: Current service-connected primary disability (e.g., your current list of service-connected disabilities from your VA.gov account)

- REQUIRED: Nexus Letter for Secondary Condition establishing a connection between the service-connected primary condition and the current disability
- OPTIONAL: Statement in Support of Claim (write one for each secondary disability condition you're filing for and explain the VA Claims Insider Golden Circle for each of the four elements)

PRESUMPTIVE SERVICE CONNECTION

There are certain conditions that the VA "presumes" to be service connected, even if there's no specific nexus. So, instead of having to prove a service-connected disability, you only need to show on your DD214 that you were in an eligible location during a specific time period and that you subsequently developed a qualifying condition.

For example, the PACT Act states that if a veteran served in Bahrain, Iraq, Kuwait, Oman, Qatar, Saudi Arabia, Somalia, or the UAE—or the airspace above any of these locations—on or after August 2, 1990, it is presumed they were exposed to the following airborne particulates:

- Burn-pit fumes and smoke
- Sand and dust
- General air pollution
- Fuel, jet fuel, exhaust, and mechanical fumes
- Smoke from oil-well fires

Below is a list of various PACT Act claims (sorted alphabetically) that are now presumed to be service connected:

- Asthma, code 6602 (cannot have been diagnosed before discharge)
- Brain cancer, code 8002
- Chronic bronchitis, code 6600
- Chronic obstructive pulmonary disease, code 6604
- Chronic rhinitis, code 6522
- Chronic sinusitis, codes 6510–6514
- Constrictive or obliterative bronchiolitis, code 6600
- Emphysema, code 6603
- Gastrointestinal cancer, code 7343
- Glioblastoma, code 8002 or code 8021
- Granulomatous disease, code 6524
- Head cancer, various codes
- High blood pressure (hypertension), code 7101
- Interstitial lung diseases, various codes
- Kidney cancer, code 7528
- Lymphoma of any type, code 7709 or code 7715
- Melanoma, code 7833
- Monoclonal gammopathy of undetermined significance (MGUS), code 7712
- Neck cancer, code 6819
- Pancreatic cancer, code 7343
- Pleuritis, code 6845
- Pulmonary fibrosis, code 6825
- Reproductive cancer, code 7628 or code 7528
- Respiratory cancer, code 6819
- Sarcoidosis, code 6846

Although you are not required to provide a nexus to establish a presumptive service connection, it's highly recommended you at least write a personal statement as to why you think your disability meets the legal requirements for presumptive service connection. You might want to obtain a Nexus Letter if your claim was previously denied.

The following are the evidence requirements for a presumptive service connection:

- REQUIRED: DD214 with evidence of qualifying service during the qualifying period
- REQUIRED: Diagnosis of a current presumptive disability in a medical record (STRs, VA medical records, or private medical records)
- OPTIONAL: Statement in Support of Claim (write one for each presumptive disability condition you're filing for and explain the VA Claims Insider Golden Circle for each of the four elements)
- OPTIONAL: Buddy Letter (if you're trying to prove you served at a specific location during the qualifying period or exposure to x, y, and z and it's not already documented on your DD214 and/or STRs)

SERVICE CONNECTION BY AGGRAVATION

Sometimes, military service worsens a preexisting condition beyond its natural progression. For example, a veteran may have had flat feet prior to entering the service, but wearing military boots and prolonged standing worsened the condition beyond its natural progression, leading to a painful disability called plantar fasciitis, which is eligible for compensation under the law.

Let me give you another example. If a veteran has a service-connected knee condition that aggravates a non-service-connected back condition that was preexisting, they could get service connection for their back based on aggravation—provided they can prove their condition was worsened beyond its natural progression by military service or by the service-connected disability it is secondary to.

The following are the evidence requirements for service connection by aggravation:

- REQUIRED: DD214
- REQUIRED: Diagnosis of the current VA disability you're attempting to link by aggravation to a service-connected disability (must be documented in a medical record)
- REQUIRED: Current service-connected primary disability (e.g., your current list of service-connected disabilities from your VA.gov account)
- REQUIRED: Nexus Letter for a Secondary Condition by Aggravation establishing a connection between the service-connected primary condition and the worsening beyond its natural progression of the current disability
- OPTIONAL: Statement in Support of Claim (write one for each secondary disability condition by aggravation you're filing for and explain the VA Claims Insider Golden Circle for each of the four elements)

SERVICE CONNECTION BY 38 U.S.C. 1151

This refers to disabilities or death that result from "hospital care, medical or surgical treatment, or examination" by a VA medical professional or facility or due to participation in a VA program of vocational rehabilitation or VA-compensated work therapy. In my experience, this type of service connection is uncommon and hard to prove, and it typically requires an accredited VA attorney to pursue. In addition, the evidence requirements for service connection by 38 U.S.C. 1151 vary depending on the unique circumstances of each case.

Regardless of which service connection you pursue, completing the online claim is only the beginning of the disability compensation process.

THE C&P AND ACE EXAMS

After you file a VA disability claim, chances are you'll be contacted and scheduled for one or more Compensation & Pension (C&P) exams by one of the following:

- VA doctor (works for the VA)
- Contracted doctor (works for a third-party company: QTC, VES, OptumServe, Loyal Source Government Services, etc.)

The C&P exam is the most important part of the entire VA disability claims process because Veteran Service Representatives (VSRs) and Rating Veteran Service Representatives (RVSRs) rely (almost) solely on the results of that exam to make their determination on your claim. That's because the exam involves an independent medical evaluation by a doctor who completes an online DBQ to:

- Confirm a medical diagnosis of a disability condition.
- Determine when the veteran's symptoms began and if there is a clear "nexus."
- Ascertain how bad the veteran's symptoms are overall (frequency, severity, duration).

For mental health claims, this exam includes documenting which of the thirty-one symptoms of mental health listed on the DBQ form apply to you.

I'll note here that ordering C&P exams for veterans who

have submitted a Fully Developed Claim (FDC) with a privately prepared DBQ is called "overdevelopment" of a VA claim, and it shouldn't happen. The RVSR could make a rating decision on the submitted DBQ alone, and ordering these exams slows down the disability claims process. But remember, the VA has to operate within the complex laws and regulations set forth by Congress.

Fortunately, some disability conditions don't necessarily require an in-person exam. In those cases, you may be scheduled for a telehealth C&P exam, which is just like an in-person exam only performed remotely over the internet, or an Acceptable Clinical Evidence (ACE) records-only review, which may involve a phone call.

I'll tell you how to ace these exams in a later chapter, but now that you know the basics of what the disability claims process requires, let's discuss how long it takes to review a claim and why.

THE EIGHT-STEP VA CLAIM REVIEW PROCESS

In general, a VSR and an RVSR from the VA will follow an eight-step process to review your claim. If you submit an FDC—which we highly recommend at VA Claims Insider—you'll likely get a VA rating decision within 140 to 160 days; if you submit a Standard Claim, you can expect to receive a decision within 160 to 180 days.

Why does it take so long? Besides C&P exams slowing down the process, more claims than ever are being submitted to the VA, especially PACT Act–related claims. Currently, there are around one million pending claims and three hundred thousand backlogged claims!

In addition, the Veterans Benefits Administration (VBA) is

having trouble recruiting and retaining quality talent, such as VSRs and RVSRs. Not only that, but their systems are broken and outdated, especially the Veterans Benefits Management System (VBMS), which is the primary system VA personnel use to review and adjudicate disability claims.

Here's a breakdown of the VA's claim-review process and how long each step typically takes:

1. **Claim Received:** If you file your disability claim online, you'll get an on-screen message from the VA after you submit the application. A week or so later, the VA will send you a letter to let you know they've received your claim. This letter will also show up in your VA.gov account, the web portal through which you manage your VA benefits.

2. **Under Review:** A VSR will review your claim. If the VA doesn't need any more evidence from you, which only happens when you submit an FDC, your application will proceed. This step normally takes seven to twenty-one business days.

3. **Gathering of Evidence:** The VSR may ask for evidence from you, healthcare providers, government agencies, or others before moving the claim to an RVSR for a decision. This is also when a C&P exam is ordered, if one is required. This step normally takes thirty to sixty business days and is typically the longest step in the VA claims process.

4. **Review of Evidence:** Once the VA has received all your evidence, they review to see whether additional evidence is required. If so, the RVSR will send the claim back to Step 3. VA claims very commonly move back and forth between phases, so if you see that happen with yours, don't worry—it's normal! You may also see some confusing back-and-forth messages inside your application, but they're typically for internal use

only. If the VA needs something from you, you'll know. This step typically takes seven to fourteen business days.

5. **Preparation for Decision:** The RVSR makes a decision on the entire VA disability claim file. The RVSR takes into account the claim application, medical records, supporting documents, personal statements, buddy letters, C&P exam results, and any other supporting information when making their determination. The RVSR then begins preparing the necessary documents to explain their reasoning in detail. This step normally takes seven to fourteen business days.

6. **Pending Decision Approval:** Once the RVSR's decision recommendation documents are in order, your claim will receive a final award approval, which usually involves a second-tier reviewing authority. This step typically takes seven to fourteen business days.

7. **Preparation for Notification:** The VA will prepare your Disability Claim Decision Letter and the supporting documentation used to make the rating decision to be mailed to you in its entirety. This step usually takes seven to fourteen business days.

8. **Claim Closed/Complete:** The VA will send you a packet by US mail that includes the details of your claim decision. You should receive this in seven to fourteen business days. If you don't want to wait for the packet to arrive by mail, you can log in to your VA.gov account and click on the link right below your full name, "Your Disability Rating," to see if anything has been added or changed. You can also view and download your VA Disability Claim Decision Letter online when viewing your closed claim.

Regardless of when you get your VA rating decision letter, make sure to read it in detail! If you disagree with some or all of the decision, you'll want to understand what you're going to challenge and why.

I'll go into more detail about how you can challenge your claim decision later in this book, but first, you need to understand how the VA's rating system works. This will help you get the rating and the thousands of dollars' worth of tax-free benefits you legally deserve.

CHAPTER 3

★ ★ ★

THE VA RATING SYSTEM

THIRTEEN MONTHS AFTER I LEFT THE MILITARY, I RECEIVED a VA disability rating of 90 percent. I didn't know what to think and just accepted it and moved on with my life. I didn't know you could be "underrated." I also thought it was a "one-and-done" process—meaning I thought that after you got a rating from the VA, that's it, and you have no recourse if you disagreed with anything or your circumstances changed. I was so wrong and lost around $100,000 of tax-free compensation and benefits because I didn't know any better.

Turns out, it's very common to be underrated by the VA. According to data compiled by VA Claims Insider, 80 percent of you reading this right now don't have the VA rating and compensation you deserve. That makes me angry, and my mission is to get you every penny you've earned for serving our country. Okay, let's go deeper into the VA rating system.

Your combined VA disability rating is incredibly important because it could be the difference between receiving thousands of dollars and millions of dollars. So, let's discuss how the VA rating system works.

THE RATING SYSTEM'S FUZZY MATH

Every service-connected disability receives a rating of 0 percent, 10 percent, 20 percent, 30 percent, 40 percent, 50 percent, 60 percent, 70 percent, 80 percent, 90 percent, or 100 percent. The higher the rating, the more benefits you receive. For example, a 10 percent VA rating is worth just over $170 per month, while a 100 percent VA rating can be worth more than $3,737 per month.

This is simple enough when you only have one service-connected disability: the rating for total disability is the same as your total rating. However, most of us have more than one service-connected disability. So, how does the VA consider all of them and wind up with one combined VA rating percentage?

If you receive several ratings for corresponding disabilities, they will not just be added together in a cumulative nature. If I am rated at 70 percent for PTSD and 50 percent for sleep apnea, I won't be 120 percent disabled. It's physically impossible to be more than 100 percent disabled. Instead, the VA starts with your highest overall rating, multiplies the next highest rating into the previous one, adds it on, and so on.

In the example I just gave, the VA would take the highest rating first, the 70 percent for PTSD. According to that number, they would assume that 100 percent – 70 percent = 30 percent of me is still "healthy." Then, they multiply that remaining 30 percent by the rating for my sleep apnea disability, which is 50 percent. Take 50 percent of 30 percent and you wind up with 15 percent. Add that 15 percent to the original 70 percent, and you wind up with an 85 percent total disability rating, which would be rounded up to a 90 percent combined VA disability rating, as the VA always rounds up or down. If you were 84 percent disabled, the VA would round that down to 80 percent. The process continues for each disability remaining from highest to lowest.

Is that clear? Clear as mud! Still, it's the system we have. Now that you understand it, you can see how someone could have five or six disabilities but if they're all low value, the rating won't reach anywhere close to 100 percent. In fact, it takes twenty-seven 10 percent disability ratings to reach a 100 percent combined VA rating.

Wondering how to increase your VA disability rating? In this book, I reveal and explain the six proven paths to getting a VA disability increase this year.

Generally, to increase an existing VA disability rating, you need to provide the VA with medical evidence showing your symptoms are worse in terms of frequency, severity, and duration. If your disabilities have worsened, you may be eligible for a ratings increase and the benefits available to veterans with a higher VA rating—one such benefit is a larger monthly tax-free compensation payment.

Scan the QR code below to learn how to increase your VA disability rating with my guide "Eight Best Ways to Get a VA Disability Increase This Year."

You may be wondering how to increase your VA disability rating all the way to 100 percent. We'll discuss that next.

THREE WAYS TO REACH 100 PERCENT

There are three paths to get a 100 percent VA rating: having a single disability rated at 100 percent, having a combined VA rating of 95 percent or higher, or being deemed unemployable. Regardless, you need to submit medical evidence that shows you have the most severe symptoms in 38 CFR Book C, Part 4, "Schedule for Rating Disabilities." In other words, you need to prove your disabilities severely impact your work, life, and/or social functioning.

Let's discuss each of the three methods to reach a 100 percent rating in greater detail.

SINGLE DISABILITY RATED AT 100 PERCENT

If you have a single VA disability that is rated at 100 percent, your combined VA rating will automatically be 100 percent. For example, if you have a 100 percent PTSD rating, your combined VA rating will be 100 percent—no need to factor in your other six service-connected disabilities.

There are many high-value VA disability claims—those that have a high likelihood of being rated at 30 percent or higher on their own. Depending on their severity, they may even be rated 100 percent. These include:

- Mental Health Conditions
- Sleep Apnea
- Migraines (Headaches)
- Plantar Fasciitis
- Chronic Fatigue Syndrome (CFS)
- IBS
- GERD
- Radiculopathy

- Peripheral Neuropathy
- Gulf War Syndrome Presumptive Conditions
- Ménière's Syndrome

COMBINED VA RATING OF 95 PERCENT OR HIGHER

If your combined VA disability rating is equal to or greater than 95 percent, the VA will round it up to 100 percent. You generally need two or three disability conditions rated at 50 percent or higher in the VA's fuzzy math calculation to reach this combined rating.

For example, the average VA rating for mental health conditions is 70 percent. Below, you can see the thirty-three ratable mental health conditions for VA disability:

- 9201 Schizophrenia
- 9208 Delusional disorder
- 9210 Other specified and unspecified schizophrenia spectrum and other psychotic disorders
- 9211 Schizoaffective disorder
- 9300 Delirium
- 9301 Major or mild neurocognitive disorder due to HIV or other infections
- 9304 Major or mild neurocognitive disorder due to traumatic brain injury
- 9305 Major or mild vascular neurocognitive disorder
- 9310 Unspecified neurocognitive disorder
- 9312 Major or mild neurocognitive disorder due to Alzheimer's disease
- 9326 Major or mild neurocognitive disorder due to another medical condition or substance/medication-induced major or mild neurocognitive disorder

- 9400 Generalized anxiety disorder
- 9403 Specific phobia; social anxiety disorder (social phobia)
- 9404 Obsessive compulsive disorder
- 9410 Other specified anxiety disorder
- 9411 Posttraumatic stress disorder
- 9412 Panic disorder and/or agoraphobia
- 9413 Unspecified anxiety disorder
- 9416 Dissociative amnesia; dissociative identity disorder
- 9417 Depersonalization/Derealization disorder
- 9421 Somatic symptom disorder
- 9422 Other specified somatic symptom and related disorder
- 9423 Unspecified somatic symptom and related disorder
- 9424 Conversion disorder (functional neurological symptom disorder)
- 9425 Illness anxiety disorder
- 9431 Cyclothymic disorder
- 9432 Bipolar disorder
- 9433 Persistent depressive disorder (dysthymia)
- 9434 Major depressive disorder
- 9435 Unspecified depressive disorder
- 9440 Chronic adjustment disorder
- 9520 Anorexia nervosa
- 9521 Bulimia nervosa

When combining disability ratings, you can also file for increases for disabilities that are already service connected. Just make sure you do this only if your symptoms have worsened and you think you deserve an increase by law.

INDIVIDUAL UNEMPLOYABILITY

If your disability renders you unable to maintain substantial gainful employment, you may receive the pay and benefits of a 100 percent VA rating—even if your combined VA rating is below 100 percent.

For example, a Vietnam veteran might have a 70 percent rating because they suffer from cancer due to Agent Orange, but if chemotherapy treatments and hospitalizations make substantial gainful employment impossible, they may instead be deemed unemployable. This is also known as "Total Disability Individual Unemployability" (TDIU).

A VA-accredited VSO, claims agent, or attorney can be useful in helping you secure TDIU benefits.

At this point, you may be wondering when the VA awards disability compensation and how they decide your rating. That's what we'll discuss next.

THE NUTS AND BOLTS OF RATING DECISIONS

Contrary to popular belief, the VA's policy is to award benefits whenever a claim is supported by facts and the law. VA raters even have a code among themselves: "Grant if you can; deny if you must."

The standard of proof the VA operates under is often referred to as the "benefit of the doubt" or "evidence in equipoise" rule. 38 US Code § 5107(b) states that when the evidence on a claim is in approximate balance, the decision should be made in favor of the veteran. Think of the "tie goes to the runner" rule in baseball.

This standard is less stringent than the "preponderance of the evidence" standard used in most civil cases, where the claimant must prove that something is more likely than not true. It's designed to recognize the difficulties veterans may face in obtaining evidence for events that occurred under the unique conditions of military service.

Other terms you may hear:

- Relative Equipoise: When the evidence persuades the decision-maker that the fact is as likely as not.
- Affirmative Evidence to the Contrary: The evidence against the matter is of greater weight, meaning the fact is unlikely.
- Clear and Convincing: The fact finder has reasonable certainty of the truth of a fact.
- Clear and Unmistakable: The evidence must establish the fact without question.

Assuming the VA decides to award you disability compensation, they will use the following rules to help determine your rating.

AVOIDANCE OF PYRAMIDING

The VA has a rule against "pyramiding," which refers to the practice of rating the same disability or the same symptoms under multiple diagnostic codes. This rule is designed to prevent veterans from receiving multiple compensations for the same disability or symptom.

According to VA regulations, particularly 38 CFR § 4.14, the principle of avoiding pyramiding is outlined as follows:

- Do Not Duplicate Ratings: A veteran cannot receive multiple disability ratings for the same symptom or for conditions that are essentially the same. For example, you aren't supposed to receive VA ratings for both GERD and IBS since the symptoms associated with each disability are so similar.

- Rate Different Symptoms Separately: However, if a veteran has multiple symptoms or conditions that are distinct from one another and not overlapping, each of those conditions can be rated separately. For example, if a veteran has a service-related knee injury that causes mobility issues and separate service-related hearing loss, each of these conditions would be rated separately because they are distinct disabilities.

The rule against pyramiding is intended to ensure fairness and accuracy in the disability rating system. It prevents the overestimation of a veteran's level of disability, but at the same time, it doesn't preclude veterans from receiving appropriate ratings for distinct disabilities that result from their service.

SEVERITY OF SYMPTOMS

When you file a claim, you need to show that your disability is negatively affecting your work, life, and/or social functioning. The VA will not provide you with monthly compensation just because you were injured, but they will compensate you if that injury continues to negatively affect you.

You'll need to have a powerful argument that there are persistent and recurring symptoms that impact you, known as "Severity of Symptoms." Maybe you've had to take all your sick days at work because of your migraine headaches. Maybe your PTSD is creating anger issues that have put your job in jeopardy.

The severity of your symptoms has a direct correlation to the rating you receive, so it's up to you to argue their severity in a compelling and effective way. You'll want to write a strong personal statement for each disability condition you're claiming using VA Form 21-4138, Statement in Support of Claim.

You can search 38 CFR Book C, Part 4, "Schedule for Rating Disabilities," for the name of your disability and your approximate symptoms. Make sure to be descriptive and use specific examples that apply to the ratable symptoms for that disability.

PREPONDERANCE OF THE SYMPTOMS

A big misconception among veterans is that you need to meet ALL the subjective mental health symptoms tied with a certain rating in order to get that rating. This is NOT true! The VA rater will consider all the evidence of record and will normally assign a VA rating for mental health based on "Preponderance of the Symptoms."

For example, if a veteran has three of the symptoms from the 50 percent VA rating for PTSD and five of the symptoms from the 70 percent rating, the rating agency will assign the higher rating, unless evidence of record contradicts this subjective assessment. The opposite is also true. If a veteran has five of the symptoms from the 30 percent VA rating for PTSD and three of the symptoms from the 50 percent rating, the rating agency will assign the lower rating, unless evidence of record contradicts this subjective assessment.

According to 38 CFR Book C, Part 4, "Schedule for Rating Disabilities," § 4.126, "Evaluation of Disability from Mental Disorders," the VA rater is required to follow these regulations:

1. "When evaluating a mental disorder, the rating agency shall consider the frequency, severity, and duration of psychiatric symptoms, the length of remissions, and the veteran's capacity for adjustment during periods of remission. The rating agency shall assign an evaluation based on all the evidence of record that bears on occupational and social

impairment rather than solely on the examiner's assessment of the level of disability at the moment of the examination."

2. "When evaluating the level of disability from a mental disorder, the rating agency will consider the extent of social impairment, but shall not assign an evaluation solely on the basis of social impairment."

PAINFUL MOTION PRINCIPLE

As we've discussed, you ideally should file for mostly high-value disabilities, but the VA also awards ratings for musculoskeletal conditions, even if a veteran does not have a specific diagnosis or their range of motion is not severely limited. That's because 38 CFR § 4.59 provides that veterans experience functional loss due to pain. The minimum compensable rating for musculoskeletal conditions is usually 10 percent.

The VA evaluates a veteran's pain during C&P exams, when the veteran is asked to perform movements or articulate when and how the pain occurs. The examiner notes the onset of pain and whether it affects the functional use of the body part. In addition, the VA may consider objective evidence, like medical records and diagnostic tests, to understand the full scope of the disability.

This is not always necessary, though. The VA recognizes that pain itself can be a ratable symptom, even if that pain cannot be easily categorized or diagnosed using traditional medical imaging or diagnostic techniques. This is a significant acknowledgment—one that allows more veterans to receive the compensation they deserve for their honorable service.

NO PROHIBITION AGAINST
CLAIMANT'S RECOLLECTIONS

In most cases, medical diagnoses and opinions are based to some degree on history provided by the veteran. Their self-interest in the outcome of a medical assessment and ability to recollect facts over time both raise concerns about whether their history is accurate—and therefore whether these medical assessments are valid.

However, as a general principle, unless the historical facts upon which a medical conclusion is based are dubious or untenable, the medical conclusion is accepted as credible. The probative value of this medical evidence is considered and weighed relative to other evidence submitted in the claim.

An exception to this rule is when a physician's conclusion merely echoes the reported history of a claimant without offering any medical rationale in support. This cannot be deemed an adequate medical opinion and, as a result, is not assigned any probative value.

At this point, you may be wondering how far back you'll be compensated after you receive your disability rating. Well, it depends on the effective date of your claim.

EFFECTIVE DATES

After the VA decides it will pay you benefits based on your disability claim, it assigns an "effective date" for your back pay. The effective date varies based on the type of benefit you applied for and the nature of your claim.

If you begin a claim more than a year after the end of your active service, the effective date is whichever of these is later:

- The date the VA received your intent to file

- The date you were first afflicted by your illness or injury (also known as the date your entitlement arose)

For example, Mike ended his active service on September 30, 2012, with a hearing disability. He filed a claim for his hearing problem on November 15, 2015. On March 10, 2016, the VA awarded Mike a 30 percent disability rating with an effective date of November 15, 2015—the date they received the claim.

However, if the VA receives your claim within one year of the day you leave active service, the effective date is:

- The day after the date of your separation from the military
- The date you were injured or diagnosed with an illness

For example, Rick ended his active service on September 30, 2014, with migraines. He filed a claim for the illness on July 5, 2015. Because the VA received Rick's claim within one year of his separation from active service, the VA awarded him a 30 percent disability rating with an effective date of October 1, 2014—the day after Rick's separation from the military.

Kim separated from active service on September 30, 2013, and received a medical test on April 15, 2014, that showed she had hypertension (high blood pressure). Less than three months later, on July 1, 2014, she filed a claim, and the VA determined her disability was service related. Because the VA got the claim less than one year after Kim separated from active service, the effective date was April 15, 2014—the date her illness was first diagnosed.

A few special cases:

- Disability Increase Claims: When a veteran files a claim for an increase in their disability rating, the VA will retroactively apply the increased rating to the earliest date that the veteran can demonstrate there was an increase in their disability. This means that the veteran may receive additional benefits dating back to the time when their disability worsened. However, there's a condition attached: the veteran must submit the new claim request within one year of the date when their symptoms worsened. If the claim is submitted within this one-year window, the VA will consider retroactively adjusting the disability rating to reflect the increased level of impairment. Otherwise, the effective date is the date the VA received the claim.

- Error in a Previous Decision: If the VA finds a Clear and Unmistakable Error (CUE) in a previous decision, the effective date of the new decision will be the date from which benefits would've been paid if there hadn't been an error in the prior decision.
- Difference of Opinion: A decision that's based on a difference of opinion will have an effective date of the original decision, if it is favorable.

This all assumes you meet the requirements of the Caluza Triangle. Simple enough, right? Of course not.

I'm sure you have several questions I haven't yet addressed, so before we talk strategy, I want to answer the questions I hear over and over again from veterans. That way, you can begin your disability claim with confidence.

CHAPTER 4

★ ★ ★

FREQUENTLY ASKED QUESTIONS

THROUGH HELPING TWENTY-FIVE-THOUSAND-PLUS VETER-ans with their VA disability claims since 2016 and spending over ten thousand hours researching and studying, I've learned a ton about the VA disability compensation system. One of the biggest things I've learned is that the system is endlessly complex and confusing, but it doesn't have to be if you know how to ask the right questions. That's why you're reading this book!

At this point, you've been educated on the basics of the VA, the disability claims process, and the VA disability rating system, but I'm sure you still have questions. In this short chapter, I will address the questions I most frequently hear at VA Claims Insider.

WHAT IS THE DIFFERENCE BETWEEN PERMANENT DISABILITY AND TOTAL DISABILITY?

Permanent VA disability exists when it is reasonably certain, based on medical evidence, that the level of impairment will continue for the rest of your life. The VA calls this "static." It means your VA disability will not improve with time. It might get worse or stay the same, but it will not get better. For example, you can have service-connected PTSD that's been rated at 70 percent for the past twelve years and is therefore considered "permanent."

Total VA disability exists when there is any impairment of mind or body that renders it impossible for the average person to engage in a substantially gainful occupation. Keep in mind that a total disability may or may not be permanent. For example, you can have a "temporary" 100 percent total disability, such as a knee replacement, where the temporary total rating will eventually be reduced.

Keep in mind, you can have a permanent and total disability.

WHAT IS PERMANENT AND TOTAL (P&T) DISABILITY?

Often seen as the holy grail of VA disability benefits, a permanent and total (P&T) disability, according to 38 CFR § 3.340, exists when:

- Your condition is not expected to improve (static). This is the most common reason the VA grants P&T disability status.
- You lose or cannot use both hands, both feet, one hand and one foot, both eyes, or otherwise become permanently helpless or bedridden.

- You have a long-standing disease or injury that is totally incapacitating and unlikely to improve with medical treatment (static).

Your age may be considered in determining permanence, but there is no set age at which a disability becomes permanent. Whether you're thirty-five or seventy-five years old, the VA rater determines whether it is reasonably certain, based on medical evidence, that your level of impairment will continue for the rest of your life.

This is the only time in VA disability benefits where the VA can take your age into consideration.

HOW DO I GET A 100 PERCENT P&T RATING?

Usually, VA raters will automatically grant you 100 percent P&T disability status if you meet the eligibility criteria. However, if you're rated at 100 percent and trying to upgrade to P&T status, you can:

1. Open a new claim online at VA.gov, and add a new disability called "Request for Permanent and Total Disability Status."
2. Upload medical evidence showing that all of your service-connected disabilities meet the definitions of permanent and total (e.g., your GERD is rated at the highest level by law and isn't going to get better, i.e., it is static).
3. Have your treating physician or other private medical professional write a letter on your behalf explaining how your disabilities meet the definitions for permanent and total.
4. Write a personal Statement in Support of Claim documenting how your disability condition(s) are static and not subject to a Routine Future Examination (RFE).

Note: A disability is considered "static" when there's been no material improvement for five years or more.

CAN THE VA REDUCE A 100 PERCENT P&T VA DISABILITY RATING?

Yes. There are four situations where the VA might reduce a 100 percent P&T rating:

- The initial 100 percent P&T rating was based on fraud.
- You have a 100 percent P&T rating but open a new claim for compensation to include Special Monthly Compensation (SMC), and the VA rater sees that one or more conditions have gotten better.
- You have a 100 percent P&T rating but open a new claim for a Specially Adapted Housing (SAH) or Special Housing Adaptation (SHA) grant, which automatically triggers a C&P exam. This means your disability conditions could be subject to a reevaluation, especially if they aren't static.
- A CUE in the original 100 percent P&T rating is found during a VA Quality Review.

WHY DOES THE VA REEVALUATE VA RATINGS?

If your disability is not considered static or permanent, the VA may reevaluate your disability rating. This is because some service-connected disabilities are expected to improve over time.

Let's say you have a mental health condition that's had a rating for less than five years and is not considered "static." The VA can reevaluate that condition within two to five years of your initial examination. This isn't necessarily a bad thing; the VA is just trying to determine if your rating should be increased, decreased, or kept the same based on the frequency, severity, and duration of your symptoms.

The following ratings are exempt from reevaluations:

- P&T VA ratings
- Disability conditions not expected to improve
- When the rating is a prescribed scheduled minimum rating

You can find whether your VA disability falls under one of these protected ratings on your VA rating code sheet.

HOW WILL THE VA NOTIFY ME OF A REEVALUATION?

The VA initiates a reexamination by scheduling a C&P exam to assess the extent to which your service-connected disability impacts your work, life, and social functioning. It is crucial you attend this appointment or reschedule it for a more suitable time. Failure to do so may provide grounds for the VA to reduce or terminate your VA disability benefits.

Remember, receiving a reexamination notice from the VA does not mean you should panic about losing your VA disability benefits. If your condition has remained unchanged, it is highly likely the VA will confirm the accuracy of your current VA disability rating and not eliminate or reduce it.

If you receive a proposed rating reduction and want to challenge it, you must provide the VA with medical evidence showing that your disability has not improved within sixty calendar days. Such evidence may include having your treating physician write a letter on your behalf, uploading specific sections of medical evidence that show your condition has not improved, or uploading other medical reports or evidence to prove your disability has not gotten better.

WHAT IS THE VA DISABILITY FIVE-YEAR RULE?

The VA disability five-year rule allows the VA to reevaluate your existing disability rating within five years (but not less than two years) of your initial examination if—and only if—your disability condition is expected to show material improvement over time. However, they may still reevaluate your VA rating past the five-year deadline if medical evidence shows your condition has significantly improved.

For example, if you have had service-connected GERD (a condition that is not "static") for the past three years with a 30 percent rating, the VA might schedule an RFE. This is essentially another C&P exam meant to assess whether your GERD has improved, worsened, or remained the same.

WHAT IS THE VA DISABILITY TEN-YEAR RULE?

The VA ten-year rule states the VA can't eliminate a rating that's been in place for ten years or more. But it can be reduced if medical evidence shows the disability has improved.

For example, you have had service-connected PTSD rated at 70 percent for the past eleven years. Medical evidence shows your PTSD has shown material improvement over time, and your current occupational/social impairment and mental health symptoms more closely approximate the 50 percent rating level. So, even though it's been more than ten years since you received your rating, the VA reduces your service-connected PTSD rating from 70 percent to 50 percent.

However, a veteran's original disability rating can be elimi-nated after ten years if the VA determines it was based on fraud.

WHAT IS THE VA DISABILITY TWENTY-YEAR RULE?

The VA twenty-year rule states that if your current VA rating has been in effect for twenty years or more, the VA can't reduce it below the lowest rating it held during the previous twenty years.

For example, you have had service-connected migraine headaches for the past twenty-two years. They have been rated at 50 percent for the past twenty years. According to the VA disability twenty-year rule, even if your migraine headaches show significant improvement, the VA can't reduce your rating below 50 percent.

Note: If your disability is deemed "static" at 50 percent, it is highly unlikely the VA will reevaluate you and lower the rating, unless the rating was based on fraud.

WHAT IS THE VA DISABILITY FIFTY-FIVE-YEAR RULE?

The VA fifty-five-year rule states that veterans are protected from future periodic reexaminations if they are over the age of fifty-five.

For example, a veteran born on March 7, 1963, claims an increase in his service-connected PTSD, which is currently rated at 50 percent. Medical evidence supports an increased rating of 70 percent, but it also indicates the veteran recently began attending weekly counseling sessions with a therapist.

The prognosis for progress is hopeful and the potential for improvement likely.

When the claim is forwarded to the rating activity for a decision in February 2017, the VA awards an increased PTSD rating of 70 percent and deems the disability "static," with no future review examination scheduled. Why? Under normal circumstances, an RFE would be scheduled for performance in February 2020, three calendar years following the rating decision. However, the veteran, though only fifty-four years old at the time of the claim's referral to the rating activity, will have surpassed age fifty-five by the time the examination is conducted. Thus, the VA cannot schedule a future examination.

IS AGE A FACTOR IN VA CLAIMS?

No! According to 38 CFR Book C, Part 4, Subpart A, § 4.19, "age in service-connected claims":

- "Age may not be considered as a factor in evaluating service-connected disability"
- "Unemployability, in service-connected claims, associated with advancing age or intercurrent disability, may not be used as a basis for a total disability rating"

The only time age can impact your VA disability benefits is if the VA is trying to determine your eligibility for 100 percent P&T disability. However, age is a factor in evaluations of disability not resulting from service—for example, for VA pension benefits.

It's important to note that disability compensation does not stop because of a veteran's age; it is for the life of the disabled veteran. In some instances, the veteran's benefits can even be passed to a surviving spouse.

As a reminder, though, benefits can be stopped, lowered, or increased based on findings of fraud or changes to the severity of a veteran's symptoms and their impact on work, life, and social functioning.

Now you know more than enough to take action. So, let's start strategizing your disability claim!

PART II

STRATEGY

CHAPTER 5

★ ★ ★

THE DISABILITY COMPENSATION APPLICATION

TO HELP ME PREPARE AND FILE MY FIRST VA DISABILITY claim application, I had a VSO representative from AMVETS help me free of charge. Overall, it was a positive experience, and my VSO helped me gather the right paperwork and prepare and file my claim with the VA. The part that was missing, however, was the strategy, education, and medical evidence.

That's why I ended up underrated after my first claim and losing close to six figures in benefits I should have received. It still makes me mad just thinking about it.

At VA Claims Insider, we believe if you get your claim strategy right, you'll end up getting the rating you deserve faster. So, in this chapter, I will walk you through each part of the application, ensuring you have all the guidance you need to win your claim.

CHOOSE YOUR REPRESENTATION

Selecting the appropriate level of representation for your VA claim is critical to getting the VA rating you deserve, but how do you decide? The short answer is: very carefully. The long answer is: it depends on your disability claim situation and the level of expertise required (e.g., first-time filer, increase claims, secondary claims, denied claims, or extra-scheduler claims).

In general, you have three options:

1. File your own VA claim online at VA.gov (represent yourself via "pro se representation").
2. Work with an accredited VSO (appoint a VSO representative with POA). Here is a list of VSOs that are colocated at VBA Regional Offices: https://www.benefits.va.gov/vso/varo.asp.
3. Work with an accredited claims agent or attorney (appoint a claims representative with POA). You can search and find accredited VSOs, claims agents, and attorneys at this link: https://www.va.gov/ogc/apps/accreditation/index.asp.

The truth is that not all VSOs are good. Some are better trained than others, and VSOs have varying levels of staff available to assist veterans. So, always ask the VSO if they have direct access to the VBMS system and if they are allowed to provide you with copies of documents from your claim(s). Not all VSOs have access to the VBMS system, and some that do have internal rules that prevent them from providing you copies of a completed C&P exam.

Scan the QR code below to learn more about how to select the best VSO for your disability claim.

I know you can handle this application process on your own, but if you want additional strategy, education, and medical evidence to help you on your VA claim journey, come join the VA Claims Insider community. It's free to start! We serve and support each other, so we will not let you fail.

Regardless of how you decide to move forward, make sure you notify the VA of your intent to file now!

NOTIFY THE VA OF YOUR INTENT TO FILE

Yes, now. Stand up and carry this book over to your computer, even if you don't have all your paperwork yet.

When you start your disability compensation claim on the VA.gov website, it will automatically open what's called a Notice of Intent to File. (VA.gov is like TurboTax for disability claims.) This notice tells the VA you're about to file a claim, but you have one year (365 days) to complete it.

Note: At VA Claims Insider, we recommend only filing FDCs because Standard Claims don't require you to attach all of your supporting evidence. Instead, the VA tracks down important personnel and medical records for you, which is a recipe for denial. Maintain control by providing the VA everything they need to make a rating decision.

Crucially, in most situations, the effective date for your disability compensation will be calculated based on the date of your Notice of Intent to File. This means when all is said and done, the compensation you receive will be backdated to today (or the date of your Notice of Intent to File) rather than when you actually finish filing however many months from now. So, get started!

Later in this book, we'll talk about filing a Supplemental Claim for things like pension benefits and Dependency and Indemnity Compensation (DIC), but don't wait to begin your claim for disability compensation. Opening the online application is very intuitive and easy, and it will only take a few minutes.

If you need additional support, you can scan the QR code below to join me on screen for a free seventeen-step VA.gov tutorial.

You can also apply by mail via a form available on VA.gov, by calling the VBA at 1-800-827-1000 and asking them to open a Notice of Intent to File for you, by showing up to a regional VA office near you, or—as mentioned—by working with an accredited representative at DAV, AMVETS, VFW, American Legion, or other accredited VSO organizations.

FIGURE OUT YOUR CLAIM STRATEGY

Before you start submitting documents to the VA, you should figure out your claim strategy. At VA Claims Insider, we have a few recommendations that make the process easier for you and faster for the VA. After all, we want you to win!

LIST ONE TO THREE DISABILITY CONDITIONS PER CLAIM

Think simple, simple, simple, and LESS is MORE! More is not more. The more disability conditions you file for, the longer it will take the RVSR to review and rate your claim. The VA-claims backlog is bad and getting worse every day. As of this writing, there are around one million pending claims and three hundred thousand backlogged claims! An extremely focused strategy helps you skip to the front of the line and get a more accurate VA rating decision faster. You can always open a new claim later and add more conditions. Remember, the VA claim process is never over unless you quit! The only time I recommend adding all conditions to your disability claim is if you're pursuing the Benefits Delivery at Discharge (BDD) program or you're a first-time claim filer.

CLAIM ONLY HIGH-VALUE CONDITIONS

Remember, you're fighting against the VA's fuzzy math. If you're trying to increase your VA rating, you want to focus your strategy on high-value claims only. A high-value VA claim is a disability condition that has a high likelihood of being rated at 30 percent or higher on its own. This will give you the best chance of getting a combined VA rating increase, which means more tax-free compensation and benefits for you and your family for life! Focus on mental health claims, simple increase claims, and/or secondary claims only.

BE THOROUGH AND ACCURATE

If you've never filed a VA disability claim before, there are several documents and items of personal information you can submit that you may not have considered but that could help your claim. These include your:

- DD214 (discharge papers)
- Social Security number—This becomes your VA file number in most cases
- Full name, mailing address, email address, and phone number
- Direct deposit account—This can be submitted on VA.gov or by calling 1-800-827-1000.
- STRs, VA medical records, and/or private medical records— It's NOT enough to say you have a condition. You must have a current medical diagnosis (within the last twelve months or documented continuation of treatment). If you have a disability condition but don't have it diagnosed yet, get your butt to the doctor!
- Nexus Letter from a private healthcare provider if your claim was previously denied
- Buddy Letter from someone eighteen years of age or older who witnessed the in-service event or injury and can shed light on the condition currently affecting you. (Visit the VA Claims Insider blog for more tips on how to write a Buddy Letter.)
- Complete a Statement in Support of Claim (VA Form 21-4138), a written personal statement about your symptoms and how those symptoms are negatively impacting your work, life, and social functioning.

The mind-boggling thing is none of these items are technically "required to file a claim." In fact, some of them won't even be suggested. Just because the VA doesn't ask for it, however, doesn't mean you shouldn't include it. Heck, this is part of why I wrote this book for you. We make VA claims easy!

GET COPIES OF YOUR STRS AND MEDICAL RECORDS

Service Treatment Records (STRs) are your military medical records. They contain your full military medical history, including your diagnosis history, and they are a critical part of achieving VA claim victory!

There are three main ways to obtain copies of your STRs:

- If you're working with an accredited VSO, ask them to download .pdf copies of your STRs from VBMS and send them to you.
- Go to a VBA regional office in your state, talk to a representative in person, and have them print copies of your STRs for you.
- Get a copy of your VA Claims File (VA C-File); it will include copies of your STRs (this can take ten to fourteen weeks or longer).

To download complete copies of your VA medical history:

1. Navigate to the MyHealtheVet website at https://www.myhealth.va.gov/.
2. Click the "Sign in" button located at the top-right corner of the homepage. Select your sign-in method as there are multiple ways to log in.
3. Once you've signed in, click the link that says, "Blue Button Medical Reports."
4. Click the link that says, "VA Blue Button Report."
5. Select the date range you want, and then click the radio button that says, "All Types of Information."
6. Scroll down to the bottom of the page and click the blue button that says, "Submit."

7. Find the larger of the two files listed on the screen and click the link that says, "Download PDF."
8. Click "Okay," and your VA medical records will begin to download in .pdf format.

Note: You can file a disability claim without your STRs and medical records. VSRs and RVSRs have a legal "duty to assist" and will get your STRs for you. However, filing without your STRs and full necessary medical records will automatically bump you from an FDC to a Standard Claim—and an FDC is preferred because YOU maintain control.

GET A COPY OF YOUR VA CLAIMS FILE (VA C-FILE)

Your VA C-File contains all the supporting evidence considered and rating decisions made by the VA for every VA claim you've filed. If you think about a large filing cabinet with multiple drawers, an individual VA claim you've filed would be one drawer in the cabinet, whereas your VA C-File IS the cabinet (all the drawers and files). While an individual claim might be hundreds of pages, a veteran's VA C-File is usually a thousand pages or more.

If you've previously submitted a claim, you should obtain a copy of your VA C-File to review previous evidence considered by the VA and ensure the accuracy of prior VA rating decisions. If you've had a VA claim denied, it is critical to know what evidence was reviewed and considered by the VA in the denial.

View the evidence carefully, as it will help you form a better VA claim strategy for future claims.

The VA C-File includes:

- VA Form 21-526EZ, Application for Disability Compensation and Related Compensation Benefits
- DD214, Certificate of Release or Discharge from Active Duty
- STRs
- Military Personnel File
- VA Medical Records
- Private Medical Records
- DBQs
- Nexus Letters
- Statements in Support of Claim
- VA Buddy Letters
- C&P Exam Results (to include private contractor C&P exam results)
- Disability Claim Decision Letters
- Appeals (prior Notices of Disagreement, HLRs, Supplemental Claims, Board Appeals)
- Internal VA Correspondence

Note: Due to the current VA claims backlog, if you request your VA C-File from the Department of Veterans Affairs Evidence Intake Center, turnaround times can be more than fifty-two weeks. If you're lucky, it might only take eighteen to twenty-four weeks.

GET A COPY OF YOUR VA RATING CODE SHEET

A VA rating code sheet is a document that shows all the VA disability conditions you're currently rated for (if you've previously submitted a claim). This sheet includes the diagnostic code, disability condition name, type of service connection, whether the disability is "static," the date(s) of service connection, and your current VA disability rating for each condition.

Your code sheet is especially useful if any of your VA disabilities are subject to an RFE—meaning they could be reevaluated in the future. Note: If you see the words "Static Disability" next to an individual VA disability on your VA code sheet, you will not be reevaluated.

Your VA code sheet includes:

- Veteran name
- VA file number
- Representative with POA
- Active-duty service history
- Character of discharge
- Future exam dates
- VA disability diagnostic codes
- List of service-connected VA disability conditions
- List of non-service-connected VA disability conditions
- Combat or noncombat service
- Combined VA disability rating
- Special monthly compensation entitlement
- VA pension entitlement
- Ancillary decisions
- Reviewer notes

There are two main ways to get a copy of your VA rating code sheet:

- Ask your accredited VSO to download your VA disability code sheet from the VBMS. This is the fastest (and easiest) way to get it.
- Get a copy of your code sheet by requesting your VA C-File.

Remember that the key element of your VA code sheet is it shows each disability you're rated for and whether it's "static" in nature.

AVOID GETTING DENIED

As I've mentioned, there are two primary reasons why VA disability claims get denied. The first reason is many veterans do not have enough medical evidence to prove they have a disability condition (for example, there may be no diagnosis in a medical record, especially STRs) or symptoms severe enough to warrant a VA disability rating under the law. The second reason is many veterans are unable to prove a service connection to their disability, the nexus.

So, the ultimate strategy for winning your disability claim is to provide as much evidence as possible. A big part of that, of course, is submitting all your documentation, but another part is acing the C&P exam.

CHAPTER 6

★ ★ ★

THE COMPENSATION & PENSION EXAM

BECAUSE I HAVE MULTIPLE DISABILITIES AND FILED MULTIPLE VA claims throughout the years, I've undergone around ten C&P exams over the last eight years. Though they were mostly successful, not one of these exams made me feel comfortable. I have trouble trusting people in general, and the examiner holds so much power.

The C&P exam is understandably scary for veterans. Somebody you don't know, who's never treated you, conducts an examination that will likely determine the amount of your VA disability benefits—the benefits that you deserve to help support yourself and your family. You can do everything else right, but if you miss your C&P exam or, worse, have a bad C&P exam, the results can ruin your final VA rating. It's shameful, I know, but the sad reality is that the VA rater, the RVSR, will rely almost completely on the notes from the C&P examiner to judge your claim.

Yeah, that's scary.

One of the questions I get asked all the time is, "Brian, do you have any C&P exam tips?" Yes, I do! Because, in my opinion, the C&P exam is the most important day in the entire VA claim process; it's best to overprepare. So, let me tell you more about what to expect and how to get ready.

OVERVIEW OF THE C&P EXAM

Regardless of how much information you provide in your claim, the VA will likely order a separate medical examination from a medical provider contracted to work for the VA. This is the C&P exam. You'll likely get a phone call and a packet in the mail with instructions. Some exams happen over the phone or via video teleconference, while others are required to be conducted in person. Some might even happen based on a records review alone, which is known as an ACE exam.

As a reminder, the C&P exam is an evaluation of a veteran's claim for service-connected disability compensation or for an increase in their disability rating. It's conducted by a private examiner on behalf of the VA when there's insufficient medical evidence to support the claim or when the VA needs more information to determine the extent of the disability, its connection to military service, the existence of a disability secondary to a service-connected disability, or the appropriate compensation level.

The C&P exam is not a full physical evaluation nor is it for diagnosis or treatment of medical conditions. Instead, the administrative exam consists of a series of questions aimed at understanding the extent and impact of the veteran's disability. This helps determine the disability rating, which influences the type of compensation the veteran receives from the VA.

Specifically, the examiner fills out the DBQ, an online form used by the VA to evaluate the severity and impact of a veteran's disability. The DBQ form is specific to a certain type of medical condition or body system and includes questions about the severity of symptoms, the degree of functional impairment, and the impact of the condition on the veteran's daily life. For instance, there are separate DBQs for orthopedic conditions, mental health conditions, and respiratory conditions.

The length of the exam varies, usually lasting fifteen to twenty minutes for non-mental-health claims and one hour for mental health claims but can be longer depending on the complexity of the conditions being evaluated. Following the exam, the examiner writes a report that includes their findings, which is then used by the VA to make a decision on the claim.

It's crucial for veterans to attend their C&P exam. Missing the appointment without a valid reason can lead to denial of the claim or a decrease in benefits. If a veteran cannot attend, they should inform the VA as soon as possible and reschedule.

Now, on to my tips!

READ THROUGH YOUR MILITARY, VA, AND PRIVATE MEDICAL RECORDS

Do this in detail prior to your C&P exam.

There is no substitute for knowing what's in your STRs, VA medical records, or private medical records.

Be prepared to discuss the medical diagnosis of your disability, any subjective ratable symptoms of your disability that are in your medical records, and the logical link or connection between your current disability and your active-duty military service—the nexus.

When did the symptoms of the disability begin?

Did they start on active duty or after you left the service?

Do you have current ratable symptoms of the disability into the present day?

If yes, how severe are those symptoms?

Know the answers to all these questions.

REVIEW 38 CFR BOOK C, PART 4, "SCHEDULE FOR RATING DISABILITIES"

The law that governs all VA disability claims is 38 CFR Book C, Part 4, "Schedule for Rating Disabilities" (also known as the "VASRD").

The complete VA disability claims list contains 834 ratable disabilities under the law.

You should review the general schedule prior to your C&P exam, which will help you understand your disability and how your current ratable symptoms and keywords are tied to a specific rating under the law.

You should also review the condition-specific DBQ for your claimed disability; this is what the C&P examiner will complete online at your exam.

One of our websites, militarydisabilitymadeeasy.com, has categorized the entire VASRD with "simple" and "made easy" answers.

CREATE A DETAILED PLAN FOR EXAM DAY

Before your exam, consider the following questions:

- Where is the location of your C&P exam?
- What are you going to wear?
- What are you going to bring with you?

- Do you require the assistance of devices like braces or walkers?
- Are you going to bring another person with you to the C&P exam?
- How do you feel on exam day?

Make sure to get to your exam at least thirty minutes early. Check in with your photo ID and begin completing any questionnaires given to you. Write down the doctor's name and date/location of the exam; you may need it later if you DISAGREE with the exam results (keep copies of the C&P exam notification paperwork sent to you by US mail).

DO NOT DESCRIBE YOUR BEST DAY

You need to tell the C&P examiner how you are on your very worst days.

Remember that the VA C&P exam is a snapshot in time of how you're doing on one particular day.

If you're having a good day, but this is unusual for you, make sure to explain to the examiner how you normally are on your worst days.

For example, if your back pain is so severe you often can't get out of bed in the morning without help or you wear a back brace, make sure to tell the C&P examiner these things in detail.

MISSION CRITICAL: Don't ever lie or stretch the truth when it comes to your VA disability claim.

That's illegal.

At your C&P exam, you should think, look, act, and speak as you would on a normal day.

What does this mean?

Here are a few examples:

If you don't require the daily use of braces or a walker, don't just pull them out for your C&P exam. Do what you would normally do.

If you usually shower and dress decently, do so on the day of your exam. We recommend you wear comfortable clothing, such as sweatpants and a T-shirt. If you're reporting to the exam from work, wear what you normally wear for work.

If you're able to lift weights and work out, tell the examiner the truth. Don't say you can't lift more than ten pounds if you're at the gym using forty-pound dumbbells.

A C&P examiner might write that you're malingering if you attempt to falsify or exaggerate your disability symptoms/impairment. The VA defines "malingering" as "the intentional production of false or grossly exaggerated physical or psychological symptoms motivated by external incentives such as avoiding military duty, avoiding work, obtaining financial compensation, etc."[8]

Important: according to federal law, there are criminal penalties, including a fine and/or imprisonment for up to five years, for withholding information or knowingly providing incorrect information in support of your VA disability compensation claim for VA benefits (18 U.S.C. § 1001).

BE "UNCOMFORTABLY VULNERABLE"

If it feels uncomfortable for you to say something to a C&P examiner you just met, that means you need to say it!

---

8   No. 1637610, Docket No. 12-27 035 (Board Vet. App. Sept. 26, 2016), https://www.va.gov/vetapp16/Files5/1637610.txt.

For example, nobody wants to talk about their sexual dysfunction, and that's exactly why you need to talk about it.

Tell the C&P examiner about the severity of your ED and how it's hurting your relationship with your spouse.

If you're abusing alcohol as a coping mechanism because of your severe anxiety and insomnia, you should tell the examiner. You're helping explain the severity of your mental health symptoms by saying, "I'm abusing alcohol and drugs to numb the pain and escape my anxiety and depression."

EXPLAIN THE SEVERITY OF YOUR DISABILITIES

VA claims for all mental health conditions come down to your current level of "Occupational and Social Impairment" as well as the severity of your mental health symptoms and circumstances.

How is your severe PTSD affecting your work, life, and social functioning?

VA claims for other conditions (non-mental health) are all about six things:

- Limitation of range of motion
- Pain level
- Loss of use
- Economic impact
- Frequency
- Duration

Make the examiner stop as soon as you feel any pain or discomfort.

If you can't bend over to touch your toes, don't do it! If you're unable to move your knee to your chest, don't let the examiner move you!

Be prepared to discuss how your disability is limiting and affecting your work, life, and social functioning.

For example, you can say things like, "My PTSD is so severe I had an angry outburst at my boss last week and got written up for it."

Another example is, "My plantar fasciitis is causing me so much heel pain that I can no longer run or work out, and I've gained twenty pounds in the past three months. In fact, it's difficult to walk, and shoe inserts don't help."

KNOW YOUR TRUE STORY COMPLETELY

Be prepared to discuss many related incidents in detail with the examiner. Most veterans don't have specific incidents well documented, so make sure to discuss the approximate month and year your disability symptoms began.

You may want to include a VA Buddy Letter to help explain and corroborate your story, which will help prove the nexus requirement for service connection.

For example, "I was sexually assaulted by my boss on a navy ship in October 1987. I never told anyone about this incident, as I feared for my life and career."

You must also be prepared to talk about your life before, during, and after your service in detail. For example:

- Where did you grow up, and what was your life like before joining the military?
- What did you do on active duty, and did you have any specific job requirements?
- Did you deploy to a combat zone or other austere location?
- What happened after you left active-duty service?

Make sure you've given the C&P examiner a detailed picture of how the military either caused or made your disability condition worse, or how your service-connected disability caused or aggravated your currently claimed disability. If you can make the C&P examiner feel something, they'll be able to relate to your story, which will help them make the proper analysis regarding the severity of your disability.

DO NOT BEFRIEND THE C&P EXAMINER

Keep in mind that the C&P examiner is NOT your friend. The examiner is there to do a job they're being paid for, which is to conduct an adequate examination of your claimed disability and document the record for the VA rater.

You are also there to do a job, which is to be open, honest, truthful, and uncomfortably vulnerable. Be polite and courteous during the exam, but stay away from small talk.

And remember this: your VA C&P exam begins when you pull into the parking lot!

BRING HARD COPIES OF YOUR DOCUMENTS

I get asked this all the time: "Brian, I have trouble remembering things; can I bring my medical records, Nexus Letters, DBQs, and personal statements to the C&P exam?"

The answer is YES!

Review them before the exam, and put them in a folder to bring to the exam. It's also okay to offer them to the C&P examiner, but don't force it.

The C&P examiner should have already reviewed all your submitted evidence (digitally) before your C&P exam, but sometimes they are lazy, aren't prepared, and haven't reviewed the documents the VA sent them or the VA did not send them all the documentation.

So, yes, it's a good idea to have your hard-copy evidence with you and offer it to the examiner.

Take note that if you bring new records to your exam not previously submitted, the provider may review them, but they can't submit records for you.

After your exam is over, you can also leave copies of your evidence with the examiner for further review and analysis, if they choose to accept them.

DOWNLOAD YOUR C&P EXAM RESULTS

This final tip is critical, especially if you think you might have had a bad C&P exam.

You can challenge the accuracy and validity of your C&P exam, including requesting a new exam BEFORE your final VA rating decision, by calling 1-800-827-1000.

If your C&P exam was performed by a VA doctor at a VA facility, the results of your C&P exam will be in your VA medical records on MyHealtheVet within forty-eight to seventy-two hours after the exam.

If your C&P exam was performed by a contracted doctor at a private facility, the results of your C&P exam will be uploaded to the VBMS.

The fastest and easiest way to get your C&P exam results from a contracted provider is to have your accredited VSO download a copy for you from VBMS. Note: Not all accredited VSOs, claims agents, and attorneys have access to the VBMS system.

Finally, you can get a copy of your C&P exam results (and your entire VA claims file) by filing an online Freedom of Information Act (FOIA) request for a copy of your VA C-File.

THE VBA FOIA REQUEST FORM

You can search online for VA Form 20-10206 "Freedom of Information Act (FOIA) or Privacy Act (PA) Request."

This form is used to submit an FOIA or Privacy Act request. It must be signed by the requester or a third-party authorized to act on behalf of the requester.

Complete the form in detail and make sure to check the radio button that says, "Claims File (C-File)."

The fastest way to submit your VBA FOIA request form to get your VA C-File is to use the AccessVA QuickSubmit upload tool.

Go to the AccessVA homepage: https://eauth.va.gov/accessva/.

Once you've completed the C&P exam, make sure to congratulate yourself. You've made it through a long, complicated process, and now, all you have to do is wait to hear the VA's decision.

CHAPTER 7

* * *

THE DECISION (AND WHAT TO DO AFTER)

VA EMPLOYEES ARE HUMAN, JUST LIKE YOU AND ME, AND because of that, they sometimes make mistakes when reviewing and evaluating VA disability claims.

In fact, I've seen instances where the VA issued a rating decision to the wrong veteran.

I've also seen evidence listed in the decision that either wasn't submitted or wasn't even from the veteran in question.

I've witnessed a number of VA claim denials where critical evidence wasn't considered by the C&P examiner or the VA rater, which should be corrected in an HLR.

And sometimes, you just have a bad C&P exam and that leads to a VA claim denial or a lower VA rating than you know you deserve.

As we've previously discussed, you can usually expect to receive a VA rating decision for an FDC within 140 to 160 days, but you may not know how to obtain or interpret the Rating Decision Letter let alone what to do after the decision is made. Let's talk about that now.

THE RATING DECISION LETTER

A VA Rating Decision Letter is a document prepared by the VA rater that formally explains the VA's rationale for approving, denying, or deferring your VA disability claim. Your VA Rating Decision Letter includes the VA's final rating decision and analysis as well as WHY and HOW the VA rater and C&P examiner arrived at their opinions and conclusions for your VA claim.

The final document will be physically mailed to the home address listed in your VA.gov account, but there are three other ways to get a copy:

- Call 1-800-827-1000 and ask a VA representative to send your letter via US mail or email (if fourteen days has passed since the Rating Decision Letter was originally mailed).
- Ask your accredited VSO to download a copy of your VA Rating Decision Letter from the VBMS.
- Submit an FOIA Request via email for a complete copy of your VA C-File. Your VA C-File will contain all the VA Rating Decision Letters ever issued to you.

The Rating Decision Letter has five sections: Introduction, Decision, Evidence, Reasons for Decision, and References. I'll go over each in more detail.

SECTION 1: INTRODUCTION

This section lists your branch of service and dates of active duty from your DD214. It also lists the date the VA says it received your VA disability claim, the type of claim or appeal the decision covers, and any presumptive service that applies. Make sure this information is correct!

SECTION 2: DECISION

This section lists the individual disabilities you filed for as well as the VA rater's high-level decision regarding service connection and the disability rating he/she assigned for each condition. It's essentially the "Bottom Line Up Front" rating decision made by the VA rater.

SECTION 3: EVIDENCE

This section is very important because it lists all the evidence reviewed and considered by the VA rater. Make sure all the evidence you submitted is correct and listed in this section! While VA raters are supposed to consider all the evidence of record (everything in your VA C-File), many review and rate claims by "Top Sheeting" to save time. "Top Sheeting" occurs when a VA rater only reviews new evidence submitted since your last VA rating decision.

One common VA rating decision error made in this section is only considering some (not all) of the evidence submitted with your claim. For example, maybe the VA rater didn't receive, review, or consider your Nexus Letter, Statement in Support of Claim, or Buddy Letter before making his/her rating decision. If this happens, you should appeal using the HLR or Supplemental Claim option.

SECTION 4: REASONS FOR DECISION

This section is the most important part of your VA Rating Decision Letter because it explains the VA rater's and C&P examiner's analysis and rationale behind their final rating decisions. It also lists any favorable findings, even if the VA denied your claim. Read this section carefully!

Common VA rating-decision errors include:

- Only considering some, not all, of the evidence submitted with your claim.
- Discounting the "probative value" of a private doctor's Nexus Letter versus the C&P examiner's medical opinion (siding with the C&P examiner over your private doctor).
- Accepting the C&P examiner's medical opinion as fact based on an inadequate exam or incomplete DBQ.
- Making an illogical "less likely than not" decision for direct service connection, secondary service connection, or service connection by aggravation and denying the claim.
- Not addressing "how" the disability was aggravated by military service beyond its natural progression or by another service-connected disability when the Nexus Letter or evidence provided proves it on an "at least as likely as not" basis.
- Having the C&P examiner provide a negative medical opinion using the words "without resorting to mere speculation" when you submitted a privately prepared Nexus Letter or other credible medical evidence that did provide a link for service connection.

SECTION 5: REFERENCES

The last section includes a standard statement that 38 CFR Book C, Part 4, "Schedule for Rating Disabilities" governs entitlement to VA benefits.

THE APPEAL PROCESS

If the VA denies part or all of your claim, you have three options to appeal the decision:

1. Higher-Level Review (HLR)—START HERE FIRST
2. Supplemental Claim—THEN HERE (if HLR denied)
3. Board Appeal—RECORDS ONLY (if #1 and #2 fail)

Let's go over each of these options in more detail.

HIGHER-LEVEL REVIEW (HLR)

If you disagree with the VA's decision, you can request to have a senior reviewer take a *NEW* look at your case (normally a Division Review Officer). The reviewer will determine whether the decision should change based on a difference of opinion or error.

You are NOT able to introduce new evidence! We recommend HLR first if you have the right medical evidence, an independent medical opinion, and a description of the nexus in the denied claim. Note: Filing an HLR must be done within one year of the date of the decision.

You can do an informal phone conference or a records-only review.

You can now file your HLR online at VA.gov: https://www.va.gov/decision-reviews/higher-level-review/request-higher-level-review-form-20-0996/.

SUPPLEMENTAL CLAIM

When you choose to file a Supplemental Claim, you're able to add NEW and RELEVANT evidence NOT previously considered. A reviewer will determine whether the new/relevant evidence changes the previous decision.

- NEW evidence is information that the VA didn't have before the last decision.
- RELEVANT evidence is information that could prove or disprove something in your claim.

For example, after the VA denies service connection due to "no nexus exists," a veteran submits a new Nexus Letter from a private healthcare professional (*NEW* Nexus Letter). After the VA denies the claim because the "disability does not exist," the veteran submits a VA or private medical report showing the existence of the disability.

You can file a Supplemental Claim at any time, but we recommend you file within one year of the date on your previous denial.

You can now file a Supplemental Claim online at VA.gov: https://wwws.va.gov/decision-reviews/supplemental-claim/file-supplemental-claim-form-20-0995/.

Note: Any previously denied VA claim must be appealed as a Supplemental Claim if you are reopening the claim. This includes previously denied claims you wish to appeal under a new theory of service connection. For example, let's say you filed a claim for sleep apnea in 2017 using direct service connection, and the VA denied your claim. Now, in 2024, you want to file a claim for sleep apnea secondary to your service-connected sinusitis. Instead of opening a new claim and filing for secondary service connection, you need to file a Supplemental Claim and explain your new theory of secondary service connection.

BOARD APPEAL

When you choose this option, you're appealing to a Veterans Law Judge at the Board of Veterans' Appeals in Washington, DC. This judge, an expert in veterans law, reviews your case. You have one year from your date of decision to request a Board Appeal.

You can now request a Board Appeal on VA.gov: https://www.va.gov/decision-reviews/board-appeal/ request-board-appeal-form-10182.

With a Board Appeal, there are three different options you must choose from.

Option 1: Request a Direct Review

- If you choose the direct-review option, a Veterans Law Judge will review your appeal based on the evidence you already submitted. You can't submit new evidence, and you can't have a hearing.
- Note: The direct-review option will take an average of 365 days (one year) for the board to complete.

This is the option we recommend if you request a Direct Review (more evidence and hearings take FOREVER!). With this option, a Veterans Law Judge will review your appeal based on evidence already submitted. You can't submit evidence and can't have a hearing. This method is way faster than the other two!

Option 2: Submit New Evidence

- If you choose this option, you can submit new evidence for a Veterans Law Judge to review. You must submit this evidence within ninety days of the date they receive your request for a Board Appeal.
- Note: The evidence-submission option will take an average of 550 days (1.5 years) for the board to complete.

Option 3: Request a Hearing

- If you request a hearing with a Veterans Law Judge, you can choose to add new and relevant evidence. You can submit this evidence at the hearing or within ninety days after the hearing. Adding evidence is optional.
- The hearing will be transcribed (written down) and the transcript added to your appeal file.
- Note: The hearing option will take an average of 730 days (two years) for the board to complete.

IMPORTANT VA LETTERS

Regardless of whether you agree with your rating decision, there are multiple VA letters you should download in .pdf format from the VA.gov website. Here are step-by-step instructions:

1. Navigate to the VA.gov website.
2. Click on the "Sign in" button located at the top-right corner of the homepage. Sign in using your verified ID.me, My HealtheVet, or DS Logon account. If you don't have an account, you will need to create one and verify your identity. There is also two-factor authentication you'll need to complete to login.

3. Once you've signed in, go to https://www.va.gov/records.
4. Scroll down and click the link that says, "Download your VA benefit letters."
5. Click the green button that says, "Get your VA benefit letters."
6. Confirm your correct mailing address, and click the button that says, "View letters."
7. Select the letter you want to download by clicking the blue button that says, "Download letter."

There are several different types of letters you can download. Let me explain what each is and what you can use it for.

COMMISSARY LETTER

If you're a veteran with a 100 percent service-connected disability rating, take this letter, a copy of your DD214 or other discharge papers, and your DD2765 to a local military ID and pass office. You can schedule an appointment to get a 100 Percent Disabled American Veteran ID card at the office or use the Rapid Appointments Scheduler. The 100 Percent Disabled American Veteran ID card gives you access to your local base facilities, including the commissary and post exchange.

PROOF OF SERVICE CARD

This card shows that you served honorably in the armed forces. This card might be useful as proof of status to receive discounts at certain stores or restaurants.

PROOF OF CREDITABLE PRESCRIPTION DRUG COVERAGE LETTER

You will need this letter as proof that you qualify for Medicare Part D prescription drug coverage.

PROOF OF MINIMUM ESSENTIAL COVERAGE LETTER

This letter indicates you have Minimum Essential Coverage (MEC) as provided by the VA. MEC means your healthcare plan meets the health-insurance requirements under the Affordable Care Act (ACA). To prove you're enrolled in the VA healthcare system, you must have IRS Form 1095-B from the VA to show what months you were covered by a VA healthcare plan. If you've lost your IRS Form 1095-B, call 1-877-222-8387, Monday through Friday, 8:00 a.m. to 8:00 p.m. ET, to request another copy.

SERVICE VERIFICATION LETTER

This letter shows your branch of service, the date you started active duty, and the date you were discharged from active duty.

BENEFIT SUMMARY AND SERVICE VERIFICATION LETTER

This letter shows your service history and some of the most critical VA benefits information. You can customize this letter and use it for many things, including to apply for housing assistance, civil service jobs, and state or local property and car tax relief. Here are some of the most important pieces of information in your Benefits Summary and Service Verification Letter:

- Branch of service
- Character of discharge
- Active duty start date
- Separation date
- Current monthly compensation payment amount
- The effective date of the last change to your current award amount
- Your combined service-connected VA rating
- Whether you are totally and permanently disabled solely due to your service-connected disabilities (this is how you can verify P&T status)
- Whether you have one or more service-connected disabilities
- Whether you're receiving special monthly payments (e.g., special monthly compensation) due to your service-connected disabilities

BENEFIT VERIFICATION LETTER

This letter shows the benefits you're receiving from the VA. This letter also shows your benefits gross amount (the amount before anything is taken out) and net amount (the amount after deductions are taken out), your benefits effective date, and your current VA disability rating.

ACTIVE-DUTY ORDERS

You may be wondering what happens if you receive active-duty orders. How do you notify the VA, and how does that affect your VA disability compensation?

When you get active-duty orders, you will:

- Fill out a Statement in Support of Claim stating the dates you're on active-duty orders, the area/theater of deployment, and the unit you're assigned to.
- Attach a copy of your orders and submit them both to the VBA using QuickSubmit (or you can mail or fax them into the Evidence Intake Center of the VBA).
- Call 1-800-827-1000 and let them know you submitted the documents and are going on active-duty orders and the dates listed on your orders.
- The VBA will stop the VA compensation payments during those dates.

When you come off your active-duty orders:

- Fill out a Statement in Support of Claim stating you have come off active-duty orders. Put the area/theater of deployment you were actually in and the actual units you were assigned to. (Also include a brief recap of what duties you did that may have exposed you and may entitle you to additional VA compensation claims).
- Attach a copy of any awards/orders showing your coming off active duty and submit to the VBA using QuickSubmit (or you can mail or fax them into the Evidence Intake Center of the VBA).
- Call 1-800-827-1000 and let them know you have come off active-duty orders and you submitted a copy of the documents and the dates you were actually on active duty and you would like your VA compensation payments to resume.

The VBA will start your compensation payments the month following you coming off active-duty orders (remember, the payments are paid in the rear, so you won't get a payment until the next full month after exiting active-duty orders).

For example, let's say you are released from active-duty orders on November 15, 2023 (your active-duty pay will be subtracted from the amount you would have gotten for VA compensation pay; the VBA cannot pay you the full amount since you received active-duty pay, just like for the weeks you go on active-duty training; they subtract this amount from your VA compensation pay), your first full VA compensation payment will be on January 1, 2024.

But, as I've said before, the claims process is not over until you quit. There may be other benefits you deserve that you haven't yet looked at. Let's discuss those next.

CHAPTER 8

★ ★ ★

ADDITIONAL BENEFITS

BECAUSE OF MY SERVICE-CONNECTED DISABILITIES, MY spouse and children are eligible to receive free private healthcare for life through a VA program called "The Civilian Health and Medical Program of the Department of Veterans Affairs" (CHAMPVA).

In addition, because some of my service-connected disabilities are eligible for Special Monthly Compensation (SMC), the VA adds some extra tax-free compensation on top of my overall monthly VA disability compensation.

There are tons of additional benefits programs for veterans and their families.

While this chapter is certainly not comprehensive, it examines the most closely related benefits to VA disability claims.

Okay, let's begin.

WHAT IS THE BENEFITS DELIVERY AT DISCHARGE (BDD) PROGRAM?

If you have a service-connected condition, you can file a claim for disability benefits 180 to 90 days before you leave the military. This may help speed up the claim decision process so you can get your benefits sooner. It's also called the Benefits Delivery at Discharge (BDD) program.

To be eligible for the VA's BDD program, all of these must be true:

- You're a service member on full-time active duty (including a member of the National Guard, Reserve, or Coast Guard)
- You have a known separation date
- Your separation date is in the next 180 to 90 days (if you're leaving the military in less than 90 days, file an FDC online)
- You're available to go to VA exams forty-five days from the date you submitted your claim
- You can provide a copy of your STRs for your current period of service when you file your claim

You'll need to submit these documents with your BDD claim:

- STRs
- Completed Separation Health Assessment—Part A: Self-Assessment form
- Statements in Support of Claim (VA Form 21-4138), the name of the disability you're claiming, when/how it occurred in service, how the disability is negatively affecting you, and current severity of symptoms
- Buddy Letters to verify in-service events/incidents, how the disability is negatively affecting you, and current severity of symptoms

You are unable to use the VA's BDD program if any of these are true:

- You need case management for a serious injury or illness
- You're terminally ill
- You're waiting to be discharged while being treated at a VA hospital or military treatment facility
- You're waiting for VA to determine your character of discharge
- You can't go to a VA exam during the forty-five-day period after you submit your claim
- You didn't submit copies of your STRs for your current period of service
- You added a medical condition to your original claim when you had less than ninety days left on active duty (Note: The VA will process the added conditions after your discharge)
- You need to have a VA exam done in a foreign country, and the VA can't request the exam through the overseas BDD offices in Landstuhl, Germany, or Camp Humphreys, South Korea

WHAT IS VA SPECIAL MONTHLY COMPENSATION (SMC)?

VA Special Monthly Compensation (SMC) is an additional tax-free benefit that can be paid to veterans, their spouses, surviving spouses, and parents. For veterans, SMC is a higher rate of compensation paid due to special circumstances, such as the need for aid and attendance by another person, or a specific disability, such as loss of use of a hand or leg.

SMC-K is awarded for the loss of use of a creative organ, such as ED or female sexual-arousal disorder. The VA SMC pay rate adjusts each year with the annual cost-of-living increase.

The VA assigns SMC levels L through O based on very specific situations and combinations of situations, including, but not limited to:

- The amputation of one or more limbs or extremities
- The loss of use of one or more limbs or extremities (meaning you have no effective function remaining)
- The physical loss of one or both eyes
- The loss of sight or total blindness in one or both eyes
- You are permanently bedridden (unable to get out of bed)
- You need daily help with basic needs (like eating, dressing, and bathing), also called "Aid and Attendance"

WHAT IS HOUSEBOUND STATUS?

The VA provides various disability compensation benefits to eligible veterans through SMCs, including a little-known SMC benefit known as "housebound."

VA housebound benefits are intended for veterans who are "substantially confined" to their homes due to their service-connected disabilities. Some nonmedical indicators of housebound status may include, but are not limited to:

- Inability to walk substantial distances
- Leaving the home with assistance only occasionally for appointments, such as grocery shopping or church
- Inability to mow one's lawn

A housebound status determination also requires that a veteran is unable to leave his/her place of residence or immediate premises to earn any income.

For example, a veteran is totally disabled due to service-connected diabetes mellitus and related complications. He leaves his house weekly for dialysis treatment. His disability limits his ability to independently ambulate less than thirty feet before requiring significant rest. The veteran is entitled to SMC(s) based on housebound status. His inability to leave the home other than for medical visits demonstrates substantial confinement to his place of residence and immediate premises. Furthermore, the diabetes mellitus and complications are so disabling that he is rendered unable to leave his residence and immediate premises to earn income.

For more information on determining whether a veteran is substantially confined for the purposes of housebound determinations, see:

- *Howell v. Nicholson*
- *Hartness v. Nicholson*

Note: SMC(s) housebound is awarded in place of your 100 percent VA disability compensation. You don't get both. But, if you qualify for SMC(s), it's a higher rate of pay than 100 percent VA pay. In 2024, a housebound veteran at the single rate (no dependents) got $4,183.85 per month, whereas a 100 percent disabled veteran without housebound status got $3,737.85 per month.

WHAT ARE THE VA HOUSEBOUND REQUIREMENTS?

The housebound benefit or SMC(s) is payable under 38 U.S.C. 1114(s) (38 CFR 3.350[i]) to a veteran who has a single service-connected disability evaluated as totally disabling and:

- Has an additional service-connected disability, or combination of disabilities, independently evaluated as 60 percent or more disabling, or
- Is permanently housebound due to service-connected disability

If the veteran is entitled to housebound benefits by statute (without demonstrating need under 38 U.S.C. 1114[s]), the additional disabilities evaluated as 60 percent or more disabling must:

- Be separate and distinct from the single disability evaluated as totally disabling, and
- Involve separate anatomical segments or body systems

Notes:

- The principles regarding avoidance of pyramiding contained in 38 CFR 4.14 are applicable.
- Within these limits, the fact that the single disability, evaluated as totally disabling, and additional disabilities, independently evaluated as 60 percent or more disabling, share a common etiology does not preclude entitlement.
- In determining the eligibility for SMC benefits pursuant to 38 U.S.C. 1114(s), an erroneous disability evaluation protected by the twenty-year rule under 38 CFR 3.951(b) must be used in calculating the total percentage of disability to establish eligibility, as indicated in VAOPGCPREC 16-1989.

HOW DOES THE VA AWARD HOUSEBOUND STATUS?

A single disability evaluated as 100 percent disabling under a schedular evaluation is generally a prerequisite for entitlement to housebound benefits.

For example, you have a 100 percent VA rating for PTSD, which means you have the most severe symptoms of PTSD under 38 CFR Book C, Part 4, "Schedule for Rating Disabilities."

An exception exists in that a total disability evaluation based on individual unemployability, which is in turn awarded based on one disability, satisfies the regulatory requirement of "a single service-connected disability rated as 100 percent" for the purposes of awarding SMC housebound benefits under 38 CFR 3.350(i).

Important:

- A total rating based on individual unemployability when awarded for multiple disorders treated as one disability under the five options listed in 38 CFR 4.16(a) does not satisfy the regulatory requirement under 38 CFR 3.350(i) of "a single service-connected disability rated as 100 percent."
- The Court of Appeals for Veterans Claims (CAVC) noted in Bradley v. Peake that restrictive language precluding an individual-unemployability evaluation from satisfying the "total" requirement of 38 U.S.C. 1114(s) was dropped from the implementing regulation, 38 CFR 3.350(i), in 1995 following VAOPGCPREC 2-1994 that held that 38 U.S.C. 1114 did not authorize such a restriction.
  - CAVC only clarified in the *Bradley* decision that there was no restriction under 38 U.S.C. 1114(s) preventing the consideration of a "total" evaluation based on a service-connected disability used for individual unemployability.
  - If individual unemployability was granted based on a

single disability and the veteran has additional disabilities combining to 60 percent, SMC(s) can be granted prior to November 26, 2008, the date of the Bradley holding.

- ◦ Follow the procedures at M21-1, Part V, Subpart ii, 4.A.6.n to determine the proper effective date for entitlement to SMC based on the *Bradley* holding.

Example of TDIU award based on a single disability: A veteran is in receipt of TDIU based solely on depression evaluated as 70 percent disabling. Subsequently, service connection is granted for coronary artery disease (CAD), and a 60 percent evaluation is assigned. SMC(s) at the statutory housebound rate is awarded.

Analysis: The veteran in this instance would be entitled to the statutory SMC housebound rate. Under *Bradley v. Peake*, awarding TDIU based on the single disability of depression satisfies the requirement for a single disability evaluated as totally disabling for purposes of SMC(s) entitlement. CAD is an additional disability evaluated as at least 60 percent disabling and is separate and distinct from the service-connected depression and associated TDIU.

Here is an example of a TDIU award based on multiple disabilities. A veteran is in receipt of TDIU based on two service-connected disabilities: ankylosis of the right shoulder evaluated as 50 percent disabling and residuals of a left radius fracture evaluated as 20 percent disabling. Both disabilities are due to a motor vehicle accident (MVA) that happened during the veteran's active-duty service. He is awarded TDIU based on the disabilities caused by the MVA. The veteran's separate issue of CAD is later service connected and evaluated as 60 percent disabling. The CAD, by itself, does not render the veteran unemployable. SMC(s) at the statutory housebound rate is not awarded.

Analysis: The veteran in this instance would not be entitled to SMC(s) at the statutory housebound rate. There is no single disability evaluated as totally disabling for the purposes of entitlement to SMC. Although the evaluations for the MVA injuries to the shoulder and left radius are a single disability for purposes of TDIU entitlement, they do not represent a single disability evaluated at 100 percent disabling for the purpose of awarding SMC at the statutory housebound rate.

For more information on the single 100 percent disability requirement for SMC(s), see:

- *Bradley v. Peake*
- *Guerra v. Shinseki*
- *Youngblood v. Wilkie*
- VAOPGCPREC 66-1991

CAN I APPLY FOR VA HOUSEBOUND STATUS ONLINE?

Yes, you can apply online for a 100 percent VA housebound status via SMC(s).

If VA housebound benefits aren't automatically granted, here's how to get SMC(s) from the VA in four simple steps:

1. Open a new claim online at VA.gov and add a new disability called "Request for Housebound Status."
2. Upload medical evidence showing that your disabilities are permanently and totally disabling and meet the definition of housebound status, which requires that a veteran is unable to leave his/her place of residence or immediate premises

to earn any income. You generally need to have a single disability condition rated as totally disabling, such as a 100 percent VA rating for PTSD.

3. Have your treating physician or other private medical professional write a letter on your behalf explaining how your disabilities are total, permanent, and unlikely to improve. The letter also needs to explain that you're substantially confined to your immediate dwelling.

4. Write a personal Statement in Support of Claim documenting how your disability condition(s) are permanently and totally disabling and meet the requirements for VA housebound benefits under 38 CFR § 3.350 SMC ratings.

WHAT IS VA AID AND ATTENDANCE?

Under SMC, VA Aid and Attendance is a benefit for veterans and spouses and surviving spouses of veterans who need constant support. According to CFR Title 38 § 3.351, the veteran must:

- Be eligible for VA pension benefits
- Be so helpless that they literally require the "aid and attendance" of another person to perform the personal functions required in everyday living

Further, he or she or their spouse or surviving spouse must meet at least one of these clinical criteria:

- Be permanently bedridden, except for routine medical appointments
- Have severe visual impairment, eyesight limited to a corrected 5/200 visual acuity or less in both eyes or concentric contraction of the visual field to 5 degrees or less

- Reside in a nursing home because of physical or mental incapacity
- Require the literal "aid and attendance" of another person to perform the personal functions required in everyday living, such as dressing, bathing, eating, bathroom, etc.

Note: There are income and net-worth limitations as well.

WHAT IS "PERMANENTLY BEDRIDDEN"?

The following factors will be considered in determining the need for regular aid and attendance under 38 CFR § 3.351(c)(3):

- Inability of claimant to dress or undress himself (herself), or to keep himself (herself) ordinarily clean and presentable
- Frequent need of adjustment of any special prosthetic or orthopedic appliances which by reason of the particular disability cannot be done without aid (this will not include the adjustment of appliances that normal persons would be unable to adjust without aid, such as supports, belts, lacing at the back, etc.)
- Inability of claimant to feed himself (herself) through loss of coordination of upper extremities or through extreme weakness
- Inability to attend to the wants of nature or incapacity, physical or mental, that requires care or assistance on a regular basis to protect the claimant from hazards or dangers incident to his or her daily environment

WHAT IS "BEDRIDDEN"?

For purposes of awarding SMCs, "bedridden" is a condition that, through its essential character, actually requires the claimant to remain in bed.

The fact that claimant has voluntarily taken to bed or a physician has prescribed rest in bed for the greater or lesser part of the day to promote convalescence or cure does not suffice to qualify for SMCs.

The particular personal functions that the veteran is unable to perform should be considered in connection with his or her condition as a whole.

It is only necessary that the evidence establish that the veteran is so helpless as to need regular aid and attendance, not that there be a constant need.

Determinations that the veteran is so helpless as to be in need of regular aid and attendance will not be based solely on an opinion that the claimant's condition is such as would require him or her to be in bed. They must be based on the actual requirement of personal assistance from others.

HOW DO I APPLY FOR VA AID AND ATTENDANCE BENEFITS?

There are three ways to apply for VA Aid and Attendance:

Option #1. Send a completed VA form to your pension management center (PMC).

Fill out VA Form 21-2680 (Examination for Housebound Status or Permanent Need for Regular Aid and Attendance), which can be downloaded from VA.gov, and mail it to the PMC for your state.

You can have your doctor fill out the examination information section.

You can also include with your VA form:

- Other evidence, like a doctor's report that shows you need aid and attendance care
- Details about what you normally do during the day and how you travel places
- Details that help show what kind of illness, injury, or mental or physical disability affects your ability to do things like eat, get dressed, or take a bath

Learn about the medical evidence you'll need to support your Aid and Attendance claim and make sure to include it with your claim.

Option #2. If you're in a nursing home, you'll also need to fill out a VA Form 21-0779 (Request for Nursing Home Information in Connection with Claim for Aid and Attendance).

Option #3. Apply in person. You can also bring your printed information to a VA regional office near you.

HOW DO I QUALIFY FOR VA PENSION BENEFITS?

To be eligible for Aid and Attendance benefits you must first be eligible for VA pension benefits.

You may be eligible for the Veterans Pension program if you meet the following requirements.

Both must be true:

- You didn't receive a dishonorable discharge, and
- Your yearly family income and net worth meet certain limits set by Congress. Your net worth includes all personal property you own (except your house, your car, and most home furnishings) minus any debt you owe. Your net worth includes the net worth of your spouse.

AND at least one of these must be true:

- You started on active duty before September 8, 1980, and you served at least ninety days on active duty with at least one day during wartime, or
- You started on active duty as an enlisted person after September 7, 1980, and served at least twenty-four months or the full period for which you were called or ordered to active duty (with some exceptions) with at least one day during wartime, or
- You were an officer and started on active duty after October 16, 1981, and you hadn't previously served on active duty for at least twenty-four months.

AND at least one of these must be true:

- You're at least sixty-five years of age, or
- You have a permanent and total disability, or
- You're a patient in a nursing home for long-term care because of a disability, or
- You're getting Social Security Disability Insurance or Supplemental Security Income.

Under current law, the VA recognizes the following wartime periods to decide eligibility for VA pension benefits:

- Mexican Border period (May 9, 1916, to April 5, 1917, for veterans who served in Mexico, on its borders, or in adjacent waters)
- World War I (April 6, 1917, to November 11, 1918)
- World War II (December 7, 1941, to December 31, 1946)
- Korean conflict (June 27, 1950, to January 31, 1955)

- Vietnam War era (November 1, 1955, to May 7, 1975, for veterans who served in the Republic of Vietnam during that period; August 5, 1964, to May 7, 1975, for veterans who served outside the Republic of Vietnam)
- Gulf War (August 2, 1990, through a future date to be set by law or presidential proclamation)

WHAT IS DEPENDENCY AND INDEMNITY COMPENSATION (DIC)?

VA Dependency and Indemnity Compensation (DIC) is a VA compensation benefit provided to eligible survivors of deceased veterans.

According to 38 CFR § 3.5, DIC is a monthly tax-free compensation payment made to a surviving spouse, child, or parent of a veteran who:

- Died of a service-connected disability that occurred on or after January 1, 1957, or before January 1, 1957, if the survivor elects to receive DIC in lieu of Death Compensation per 38 U.S.C. 1310, or
- Had been rated as totally disabled due to a service-connected disability prior to his/her death, typically for at least ten years, per 38 U.S.C. 1318, or
- Died due to VA medical treatment per 38 U.S.C. 1151.

For claims based on a veteran's death in service, the effective date is the first day of the month in which the veteran died or was presumed to have died. This is true only if the VA gets the claim within one year of the date of the report of the veteran's actual or presumed death. Otherwise, the effective date is the date the VA received the claim.

If the veteran's death happened after service and the VA gets the claim within one year of their death, the effective date is the first day of the month in which the veteran died. If the death happened after service and the VA gets the claim more than one year after the veteran's death, the effective date is the date the VA received the claim.

WHAT IS THE SURVIVING SPOUSE DIC ELIGIBILITY CRITERIA?

You may be eligible for VA DIC benefits as a surviving spouse if you meet the following requirements.

One of these must be true:

- You lived with the veteran or service member without a break until their death, or
- If you were separated, you weren't at fault for the separation.

And one of these must be true:

- You married the veteran or service member within fifteen years of their discharge from the period of military service during which the qualifying illness or injury started or got worse, or
- You were married to the veteran or service member for at least one year, or
- You had a child with the veteran or service member.

Note: If you remarried, you could receive or continue to receive compensation if one of these describes you:

- You remarried on or after December 16, 2003, and you were fifty-seven years of age or older at the time you remarried, or
- You remarried on or after January 5, 2021, and you were fifty-five years of age or older at the time you remarried.

You'll need to provide evidence with your claim showing that one of the following descriptions is true for the veteran or service member. Evidence may include documents like military service records, doctor's reports, and medical test results.

- The service member died while on active duty, active duty for training, or inactive-duty training, or
- The veteran died from a service-connected illness or injury, or
- The veteran didn't die from a service-connected illness or injury but was eligible to receive VA compensation for a service-connected disability rated as totally disabling for a certain period.

If the veteran's eligibility was due to a rating of totally disabling, they must have had this rating:

- For at least ten years before their death, or
- Since their release from active duty and for at least five years immediately before their death, or
- For at least one year before their death if they were a former prisoner of war who died after September 30, 1999.

Note: "Totally disabling" means the veteran's injuries made it impossible for them to work.

WHAT IS THE SURVIVING CHILD
DIC ELIGIBILITY CRITERIA?

You may be eligible for VA DIC benefits as a surviving child if you meet the following requirements.

All of these must be true:

- You aren't married, and
- You aren't included on the surviving spouse's compensation, and
- You're under the age of eighteen (or under the age of twenty-three if attending school).

Note: If you were adopted out of the veteran's or service member's family but meet all other eligibility criteria, you still qualify for compensation.

You'll need to provide evidence with your claim showing that one of the following descriptions is true for the veteran or service member. Evidence may include documents like military service records, doctors' reports, and medical test results.

- The service member died while on active duty, active duty for training, or inactive-duty training, or
- The veteran died from a service-connected illness or injury, or
- The veteran didn't die from a service-connected illness or injury but was eligible to receive VA compensation for a service-connected disability that was rated as totally disabling for a certain period.

If the veteran's eligibility was due to a service-connected disability rated as totally disabling, they must have had this rating:

- For at least ten years before their death, or
- Since their release from active duty and for at least five years immediately before their death, or
- For at least one year before their death if they were a former prisoner of war who died after September 30, 1999.

Note: "Totally disabling" means the veteran's injuries made it impossible for them to work.

WHAT IS THE SURVIVING PARENT DIC ELIGIBILITY CRITERIA?

You may be eligible for VA DIC benefits as a surviving parent if you meet the following requirements.

Both must be true:

- You're the biological, adoptive, or foster parent of the veteran or service member, and
- Your income is below a certain amount. You can check the parents DIC rate table at VA.gov.

Note: The VA defines a foster parent as someone who served in the role of a parent to the veteran or service member before their last entry into active service.

You'll need to provide evidence with your claim showing that one of the following descriptions is true for the veteran or service member. Evidence may include documents like military service records, doctors' reports, and medical test results.

- The service member died from an injury or illness while on active duty or in the line of duty while on active duty for training, or

- The service member died from an injury or certain illnesses in the line of duty while on inactive training, or
- The veteran died from a service-connected illness or injury.

Note: If you're the survivor of a veteran who died from COVID-19 and a service-related condition made their illness worse, you may be eligible for VA DIC. When the VA reviews your application, it will consider whether a service-related condition contributed to your loved one's illness.

HOW DO I APPLY FOR DIC?

If you're the surviving spouse or child of a service member who died while on active duty, your Military Casualty Assistance Officer will help you to complete VA Form 21P-534a (Application for Dependency and Indemnity Compensation by a Surviving Spouse or Child—In-Service Death Only).

If you're the surviving spouse or child of a veteran who died while not on active duty, fill out VA Form 21P-534EZ (Application for DIC, Survivors Pension, and/or Accrued Benefits).

If you're a surviving parent of a veteran, fill out VA Form 21P-535 (Application for Dependency and Indemnity Compensation by Parent[s] Including Accrued Benefits and Death Compensation When Applicable).

Once you've completed the DIC .pdf application form, there are four ways to submit the application to the VA:

- Work with an accredited representative. This website can help you file your DIC claim: https://www.va.gov/get-help-from-accredited-representative/.
- Use the QuickSubmit tool through AccessVA to upload your .pdf application online.

- Mail your form to this address: Department of Veterans Affairs, Pension Intake Center, PO Box 5365, Janesville, WI 53547-5365.
- Go to a VA regional office and get help from a VA employee.

Now you've learned everything you need to know and more to begin applying for disability compensation and/or additional benefits. I'm excited for you to get all that you deserve for your honorable service!

CONCLUSION

THIS BOOK, MY BLOG, THE VA CLAIMS INSIDER WEBSITE, AND my entire business were born out of my own frustration with being stuck and underrated for years. I felt alone. I struggled with undiagnosed mental health conditions, substance abuse, and marital issues. Everywhere I wcnt, I felt I didn't belong. I wanted my identity back. I craved being part of a community with fellow brothers and sisters again.

After I got myself straight, I knew God had called me to *give veterans hope*. Before my books were published, there was no simple and easy-to-understand guide for navigating the VA disability compensation system. Sure, there's plenty of information freely available at your fingertips, but information alone is not helpful, especially when it's disorganized and there's too much of it. What I have tried to do here is tell you only what you need to know and then contextualize it in a way that makes sense and allows you to take action.

It is my mission to guide you through the contents of this book so you can make a change. At VA Claims Insider, we always celebrate *life change*—including not only receiving financial compensation but also overcoming addictions; finding fulfilling jobs; building stronger marriages, families, and relationships; improving physical and mental health; and becoming part of a community again. Often, these life changes start when veterans finally apply for and receive VA benefits.

When we ask veterans in our community why they haven't tried to apply for benefits yet or why they gave up trying, the number-one answer we hear is that they think they don't deserve the benefits: "I'm not disabled," or "Somebody has it worse than I do, and I don't want to take their benefits." Remember, these are lies we tell ourselves that hold us back from taking action.

This is an action book. Yes, my team and I have given you hundreds of different opportunities to receive compensation, but the most important thing we are giving you is permission to take action. There's one thing I'm sure of: if you don't take action, you won't see any results. Nobody is going to do this work for you. You need to take control of your own veteran benefits.

But I don't want to leave you hanging. At the end of this book, you'll find a list of free resources meant to help you take action, from VetNext AI to a VA Claim Secrets Masterclass. You'll also find information and tips for completing key VA forms.

You served; you deserve. You served; you earned! You earned benefits. You may not be missing a limb. Heck, you may never have deployed! But you raised your hand. You took that oath of office, and you swore to support and defend the Constitution of the United States against all enemies, foreign and domestic. Very few people do that. That journey is special. You were a part of something bigger than yourself. Sometimes, we don't realize the significance of our contribution until we're out, but the VA does—and it wants to acknowledge your service by helping you in your new civilian life and career.

My life's work is to help as many veterans as possible, but I can't do it alone. I need you to help spread the message. We need to help each other reach even more veterans and their families.

Thank you for letting me be a part of your journey. It's the highest honor of my life to serve the veteran community and give you hope. Now go open a claim already! I'll talk to you very soon.

—BRIAN REESE, US AIR FORCE VETERAN, 2003–2012

KEY VA FORMS

NOW, YOU'LL LEARN ABOUT KEY VA FORMS—WHY YOU NEED them and how to find them online.

VA FORM 21-526EZ: APPLICATION FOR DISABILITY COMPENSATION AND RELATED COMPENSATION BENEFITS

VA Form 21-526EZ, Application for Disability Compensation and Related Compensation Benefits, is required when veterans submit a claim for VA disability compensation and benefits.

Generally, VA Form 21-526EZ is one of the first and most-used VA forms for veterans filing a claim and is used for new claims, claims for an increased rating, or service connection claims.

This form requires you to include supporting documentation, including medical evidence that proves your claim, so it's crucial to have all your information together before submitting VA Form 21-526EZ.

When submitting your form, you have two processing

options: the Fully Developed Claim program (FDC program) and the Standard Claim process. The FDC program is quicker but requires you to agree that you have submitted all pertinent documentation and medical evidence and no follow-up information is needed.

However, the Standard Claim process requires the VA to obtain information to support your claim, which makes the process longer. If you choose the FDC program but the VA requires more information, they will switch you to the Standard Claim process.

Ways to submit VA Form 21-526EZ:

- Online at VA.gov
- In person at the closest VA Regional Office
- With a legal representative (a Veterans Service Organization [VSO] or VSO-accredited agent or attorney)
- Using QuickSubmit via AccessVA

By mail:

Department of Veterans Affairs
Claims Intake Center
PO Box 4444
Janesville, WI 53547-4444

VA FORM 21-4138: STATEMENT IN SUPPORT OF CLAIM

VA Form 21-4138, Statement in Support of Claim, is used when you wish to submit a personal statement—typically a three-to-five-paragraph written narrative that details the facts and circumstances of your individual VA disability condition.

While a Statement in Support of Claim isn't required, we highly recommend taking advantage of this opportunity to provide the VA with key supporting evidence. This can help complete your FDC—speeding up the claims process and increasing the chances of winning your VA claim.

VA Form 21-4138 is also especially beneficial if you lack sufficient medical evidence. This form may help you establish a service connection for a condition or a claim requesting a higher disability rating.

Here are a few tips when filling out VA Form 21-4138:

- Use as much detail as possible, painting a vivid picture of your case.
- Describe the circumstances around your accident, incident, or other related event causing your condition.
- Make your points clear, and don't add unnecessary filler information that makes it hard for the reviewer to follow your case.
- While you can add extra pages, keeping it to a few paragraphs with solid information will better support your case.
- Don't lie. You should always provide accurate information because there is a penalty of perjury for false statements on a VA disability claim.

Remember, the more relevant details you offer, the greater your chances of showing an unquestionable link between your service and your disability.

Finally, you can submit VA Form 21-4138 online at VA.gov, using the QuickSubmit tool via AccessVA, at a VA regional office, or by mail to:

Department of Veterans Affairs

Claims Intake Center

PO Box 4444

Janesville, WI 53547-4444

VA FORM 20-0996: DECISION REVIEW REQUEST: HIGHER-LEVEL REVIEW

VA Form 20-0996, Decision Review Request: Higher-Level Review (HLR), is necessary if you disagree with the VA's decision and want to request a higher-level reviewer review your claim decision. However, you can't submit any new evidence, including medical records, and you must request a VA HLR within one year from the date on your decision letter.

The reviewer will only review the evidence you submitted in your original claim, and they will determine whether an error or difference of opinion changes the decision.

In addition, unlike the Supplemental Claim Application, the VA doesn't have a duty to assist you in providing evidence to support your HLR claim or develop your case unless your HLR claim resulted in being returned to correct a "duty to assist" error in a prior decision.

Remember that once you receive an HLR decision, you can't go to the HLR again to appeal your case.

You can also schedule an over-the-phone informal conference as part of your HLR through VA Form 20-0996. This conference isn't a time to go back and forth; instead, it's a time to present your case. If you decide on a conference, it will cause a slight delay in your case.

The reviewer will contact you at the phone number you provided on VA Form 20-0996 (so make sure it's a valid number).

After attempting to contact you twice, they will review and decide your case without an informal conference.

You can quickly fill out VA Form 20-0996 online at VA.gov, using the QuickSubmit tool via AccessVA, at a VA regional office, with a legal representative (a VSO or VSO-accredited agent or attorney), or by mail to:

Department of Veterans Affairs
Claims Intake Center
PO Box 4444
Janesville, WI 53547-4444

Pro Tip: If they call to schedule your conference and the date isn't ideal, ask to reschedule. They may not always be able to handle the request, but it's worth asking.

VA FORM 20-0995: DECISION REVIEW REQUEST: SUPPLEMENTAL CLAIM

If your disability claim is denied, you can appeal the decision by submitting VA Form 20-0995, Decision Review Request: Supplemental Claim.

VA Form 20-0995 is used to file for a supplemental claim, one of the appeal options that replaced the Legacy Appeals System in 2019. You use it when you want to submit new and relevant evidence with your appeal.

New evidence refers to evidence not previously presented to the VA adjudicator with your initial claim. Relevant evidence simply refers to the evidence submitted that must prove your appeal or claim.

The VA has a duty to assist you in obtaining records to help develop your case and prove your claim. You can submit VA Form 20-0995 online at VA.gov, using the QuickSubmit tool via AccessVA, in person at a VA regional office, with a legal representative (a VSO or VSO-accredited agent or attorney), or by mail to one of the following addresses, depending on the type of benefit:

Disability Compensation
Department of Veterans Affairs
Claims Intake Center
PO Box 4444
Janesville, WI 53547-4444

Pension/Survivor Benefits
Department of Veterans Affairs
Claims Intake Center
PO Box 5365
Janesville, WI 53547-5365

VA FORM 10182: DECISION REVIEW REQUEST: BOARD APPEAL

Veterans looking to appeal their case to the Board of Veterans Appeals (BVA) must fill out VA Form 10182. By submitting this form, you are requesting a Veterans Law Judge conduct a case review of your claim.

The form requires you to list issues decided by the VA that you wish to appeal, including the decision date. In addition, you will need to include your basic information, like date of birth, Social Security number, email address, phone number, and current mailing address.

You must also select one of the three following ways for the board to review your case:

- Direct Review by a Veterans Law Judge: You aren't submitting new evidence to the board and aren't requesting a hearing. This method typically produces the fastest decision from the board.
- Evidence Submission Reviewed by a Veterans Law Judge: You have additional evidence to support your appeal.
- Hearing with a Veterans Law Judge: You request a board hearing and the opportunity to submit additional evidence to support your appeal. You will select from the following types of hearings:
  - Central Office Hearing (you appear in person in Washington, DC)
  - Videoconference Hearing (you appear from a VA regional office)
  - Virtual Telehearing (you appear virtually from an internet-connected device)

Finally, you will sign and date VA Form 10182, authorizing the Board Appeals request.

You may submit VA Form 10182 online at VA.gov, using the QuickSubmit tool via AccessVA, at a VA regional office, or by mail to:

Board of Veterans' Appeals
PO Box 27063
Washington, DC 20038

VA FORM 21-8940: VETERANS' APPLICATION FOR INCREASED COMPENSATION BASED ON UNEMPLOYABILITY (TDIU)

VA Form 21-8940, Veteran's Application for Increased Compensation Based on Unemployability, is used by veterans who can't work due to a service-connected disability and wish to apply for increased compensation.

The VA heavily relies on this form when determining appeals and claims for total disability based on individual employability (TDIU). TDIU refers to when a veteran's combined disability rating is less than 100 percent, but they can still potentially get paid at the 100 percent rate if their service-connected disabilities cause an inability to secure or follow substantially gainful occupations.

The four-page form lets the VA know more about the veteran, like their disability and medical treatment, level of education, and employment history. This includes when they last worked full time and their total earned income in the past twelve months.

In addition, VA Form 21-8940 asks when you became too disabled to work due to your service-connected disabilities.

If you require more space to list your history, a box on the last page says "remarks," where you can add additional information. You can also attach additional pages to VA Form 21-8940 to give the VA the best possible picture of your history.

However, if you don't submit the form with your TDIU claim, the VA will likely ask you to provide one; otherwise, you may receive a denied claim.

You can apply online at VA.gov, use the QuickSubmit tool via AccessVA, or mail the completed form to the following address:

Department of Veterans Affairs
Claims Intake Center
PO Box 4444
Janesville, WI 53547-4444

VA FORM 21-686C: APPLICATION REQUEST TO ADD AND/OR REMOVE DEPENDENTS

The final of the seven most common VA forms is VA Form 21-686C, Application Request to Add and/or Remove Dependents. You use this form when you want to submit a claim for additional benefits for a dependent, add a new dependent, or request to remove a dependent from your benefits.

Examples of situations where you would add a dependent include, but are not limited to:

- Marriage by ceremony
- Establishing a common-law marriage
- Proxy marriage
- Birth of a child
- Birth or adoption of a stepchild
- Adoption of a child
- Parent becoming a dependant

The following are examples of why you may wish to remove a dependent:

- Divorce
- Death of a spouse or child
- Marriage of a child
- Your child is between eighteen and twenty-three years old and isn't in school

- Removal of a dependent parent due to death

When filling out VA Form 21-686C, ensure you have all pertinent information, like the dependent's Social Security number, birth date, and place of birth. If you remove a dependent due to death, you must list the date and place of death.

In addition, if you add a student between eighteen and twenty-three years old, you must include the appropriate school name and address along with their personal information.

You can fill out VA Form 21-686C online at VA.gov or by using the QuickSubmit tool via AccessVA, and the VA will review the claim once received and notify you of their decision. You can also submit the form at a VA regional office or by mail to:

Department of Veterans Affairs
Claims Intake Center
PO Box 4444
Janesville, WI 53547-4444

OTHER VA FORMS

VA Form 21-22, Appointment of Veterans Service Organization as Claimant's Representative: If a veteran chooses to have a VSO representative help with their claim, this form is used to appoint that representative.

VA Form 21-22a, Appointment of Individual as Claimant's Representative: Similar to VA Form 21-22, this form is used if a veteran chooses an individual (such as an attorney or claims agent) to represent them in their disability claim.

VA Form 21-4142, Authorization to Disclose Information to the VA: This form allows the VA to obtain the veteran's private medical records from non-VA healthcare providers. It's essential for veterans who have received treatment outside the VA system.

VA Form 21-0781, Statement in Support of Claim for Service Connection for Post-Traumatic Stress Disorder (PTSD): Specifically for veterans claiming PTSD, this form is used to provide detailed information about the stressful events that led to PTSD.

VA Form 21-0781a, Statement in Support of Claim for Service Connection for Post-Traumatic Stress Disorder (PTSD) Secondary to Personal Assault: Similar to VA Form 21-0781 but specifically for PTSD claims related to personal assault, including military sexual trauma.

VA Form 21-10210, Lay/Witness Statement: Use this VA Buddy Letter form to capture information to support your claim from a firsthand witness, such as a family member, coworker, or someone you served with.

VA Form 10-10EZ, Application for Health Benefits: While not directly a disability compensation form, this form is used to apply for VA healthcare benefits, which can be crucial for veterans with service-connected disabilities.

VA Form 21-0966, Intent to File a Claim for Compensation and/or Pension, or Survivors Pension and/or DIC: This form is used to notify the VA of the intent to file a claim, which can help establish an earlier effective date for benefits. If you start a new claim online at VA.gov, the intent to file opens automatically.

VA Form 21P-527EZ, Application for Veterans Pension: This form is used by veterans to apply for pension benefits, which are different from compensation benefits and based on financial need.

VA Form 21-674, Request for Approval of School Attendance: Used to report a child over eighteen attending school full time, which can affect the benefits received for dependents.

VA Form 21-2680, Examination for Housebound Status or Permanent Need for Regular Aid and Attendance: This form is used when a veteran needs to apply for additional benefits due to being housebound or requiring regular aid and attendance.

VA Form 28-1900, Application for Veteran Readiness and Employment for Claimants with Service-Connected Disabilities: Use this form if you're a service member or veteran with a service-connected disability and you want to apply for Veteran Readiness and Employment (VR&E) benefits.

VA Form 10-10d, Application for CHAMPVA Benefits: For dependents of a veteran who might be eligible for the Civilian Health and Medical Program of the Department of Veterans Affairs (CHAMPVA).

VA Form 21-4502, Application for Automobile or Other Conveyance and Adaptive Equipment: For veterans applying for benefits related to automobile or special adaptive equipment due to their disabilities.

VA Form 21-4192, Request for Employment Information in Connection with Claim for Disability Benefit: This form is used to gather employment information when a veteran is claiming disability benefits based on unemployability.

BONUS RESOURCES

HERE'S A LIST OF VA CLAIM RESOURCES I RECOMMEND YOU SAVE/BOOKMARK in your favorite web browser. You'll use them a ton on your journey to VA claim victory.

CONNECT WITH A VA CLAIM EXPERT

Since 2016, the company I'm blessed to lead has personally helped more than twenty-five thousand fellow disabled veterans get the VA ratings they deserve! Will you be next?

We do this through our flagship premier program: VA Claims Insider Elite. No one pays anything up front. You only pay a fee if you get a higher rating on your disability claim that results in an increase in your disability compensation from the VA. Otherwise, the service is free. Based on that business model, you can tell we are good at what we do, or our company wouldn't still be around! We follow our eight-step VA Claims Insider Elite process based on our three-part SEM Method:

Strategy + Education + Medical Evidence
= VA Rating You Deserve Faster!

VA Claims Insider is the world's largest community of Veterans Helping Veterans Worldwide. Here's how it works. You complete a three-step intake form online, and within minutes, you'll be contacted by a veteran coach (VC) trained in our process. You'll book a strategy session to talk about your disabilities and your claim. You'll also get access and permission to use the Insider Portal, which offers access to our high-value, education-based resource library and 24/7/365 live support.

Once you have a strategy in place, we use our proprietary process to review your existing medical evidence of record and identify any gaps between your current rating and what you qualify for by law. Then, as a member, you'll receive reduced rates on our Preferred Provider Network if you need medical examinations, disability evaluation, or Nexus Letters, if and only if you want to use them. This step is optional, not required.

After you've submitted your claim, we'll provide some Compensation and Pension (C&P) exam education. Most veterans are very nervous about C&P exams. We calm nerves by demystifying the process and fully educating veterans on how to tell their full, true story.

During the claim waiting period, we are in constant contact. The veteran is never alone, whether they are joining one of our webinars or Zoom calls or just having coffee with the coaches and fellow veterans to talk. Community is key during this process. The community and level of engagement we offer and the availability of our team and resources are unmatched.

Change your life by joining us. Complete our three-step intake to start now. You'll hear from a member of our team within minutes. Visit VAClaimsInsider.com or scan this QR code:

VA CLAIMS INSIDER VIDEOS

I've spent the last ten years conducting deep research, writing, and analysis and creating specific "How-To" guides for VA Claims Insider, and now you can take advantage of our free videos. You'll learn a TON and take your game to the next level.

WEEKLY TRAINING VIDEOS

Our insider community of fellow disabled veterans have watched these videos more than three million times! We're one of the most trusted and watched YouTube channels for VA disability benefits. Our channel provides two main resources. First, we produce free, expert-level, educational, deep-dive content each week. Second, our experts go live, offering veterans an opportunity to join an event, receive answers to questions about their own claims, and get to know our experts in a more personal way.

We developed this YouTube channel because we've found that community is one of the most important things we can provide to our veterans. People want to engage not only with the material but with each other to ask questions live and participate.

Join us to find out what we're all about! Subscribe now for free at YouTube.com/VAClaimsInsider or scan this QR code to watch us free on YouTube:

VA CLAIM "SECRETS" WEBINAR TRAINING

Many of the veterans in our community tell us they prefer to learn via video training. Whether that statement applies to you or not, I strongly recommend watching my free webinar training in which I'll teach you...drumroll, please...how to win your VA claim faster and get the highest VA rating and compensation you deserve—regardless of age, income, experience, or current VA rating.

In this masterclass, you'll learn a basic overview of the disability process as well as crucial insider tips. I've organized it into three expert "secrets":

- Secret #1: THE STRATEGY: "How to Legally and Ethically Get a 100 Percent VA RATING & >$3,737/month, Tax Free, for Life (Hint: This One Is Easier Than You Might Think!)"
- Secret #2: THE LINCHPIN: "The ONE Thing You Need to Do Right Now to WIN Your VA Claim Faster (It's So Simple but Often Completely Overlooked by Many Veterans.)"
- Secret #3: THE BLUEPRINT: "How to Write Your Personal Statements & Buddy Letters the Exact Way VA Raters Want to See Them in Five Minutes or Less (Even If You Can't Write!)"

Now that you've read the book, this webinar will help reinforce the most essential pieces of information you need and motivate you to dig into your action plan. Register now! You can even watch the replay instantly at https://www.vadisabilitysecrets.com.

Or scan this QR code now to access the free training:

BLOG POSTS AND EBOOKS

Join the five-hundred-thousand-plus fellow veterans who come to our website each month to learn tips, strategies, and lessons on filing or refiling a winning VA disability claim so you can get the VA rating you deserve by law. On our blog, we go way more in depth on each of the subjects specific to disability benefits and claims.

We post a new, high-value resource each week. There's always fresh content. The blog's topics include a combination of education, medical perspective, and case law. Precedent decisions change often, so our blog is where veterans can arm themselves with the best and most up-to-date information. For example, we may post a deep dive into sleep apnea: why it's so common among veterans, how to determine whether yours is service connected, how eligibility or ratings might have recently changed, and, of course, how to successfully get a disability rating for it.

Our blog is pretty epic. I don't say that lightly. We could easily charge a monthly fee for access to this information. But we don't need to, so we don't. Learn more at VAClaimsInsider. com/Blog, or scan this QR code now:

THE ULTIMATE GUIDE TO VA CLAIMS FOR PTSD

This is arguably the most comprehensive resource ever published regarding VA disability claims for post-traumatic stress disorder (PTSD). In this Ultimate Guide, you'll learn how to get a VA rating for PTSD even if you've already filed or been denied benefits in the past. You'll also unlock the top three ways to get a VA rating for PTSD as well as critical evidence requirements, including for qualifying in-service stressor events.

Visit VAClaimsInsider.com/VA-Rating-for-PTSD or scan this QR code now to read "Top Three Ways to Get a VA Rating for PTSD: The Ultimate Guide":

THE FIVE BEST STATES FOR DISABLED VETERANS

In this post, I break down the top five best states for disabled veterans to live in using a weighted average statistical analysis. We compare metrics across the five key financial measures that matter most to disabled veterans. If you're a disabled veteran, choosing where to live after leaving the military is an important decision for you and your family. And you might be wondering, "What are the best states for disabled veterans?" Well, here's the deal: some states are more friendly to disabled veterans than others, so selecting where to live could save (or cost) you thousands of dollars per year.

Visit VAClaimsInsider.com/Best-States-for-Disabled-Veterans or scan this QR code now to read "Five Best States for Disabled Veterans (The Insider's Guide)":

TWENTY STATES WITH FULL PROPERTY TAX EXEMPTION FOR 100 PERCENT DISABLED VETERANS

In this high-value post, we list and give details on the twenty states with full property tax exemption for 100 percent disabled veterans. (Typically, you must have a 100 percent permanent and total disability [P&T] VA rating, with some limited exceptions.) Although all fifty states offer some form of property tax exemption for disabled veterans, our research and analysis uncovered twenty states with no property tax for disabled veterans at all, meaning those eligible are exempt from paying any property tax on their primary residence.

Visit VAClaimsInsider.com/Property-Tax-Exemption-for-100-Disabled-Veterans or scan this QR code now to read "Twenty States with Full Property Tax Exemption for 100 Percent Disabled Veterans (The Definitive Guide)":

THE THIRTY-FIVE BEST BENEFITS FOR 100 PERCENT DISABLED VETERANS

In this guide, I reveal and explain the thirty-five top benefits for 100 percent VA disabled veterans. We've also compiled a complete list from A to Z of little-known 100 percent disabled veteran benefits for 2024 along with tips, strategies, and lessons learned so you'll know how to get them. We even took the time to rank these benefits by importance (in our opinion) and the amount of benefit you can receive for yourself and/or your dependents. Through our experience helping more than twenty-five thousand disabled veterans, we've discovered many with a 100 percent VA disability rating don't even realize the incredible benefits available to them at the federal and state levels, from various nonprofits, and in the form of everyday military and veteran discounts, among other sources. You could be missing out on thousands of dollars of benefits you deserve for yourself and your family!

Visit VAClaimsInsider.com/Benefits-for-100-VA-Disability or scan this QR code now to read "Thirty-Five Best Benefits for 100 Percent VA Disability: The Ultimate Guide":

THE ONE-HUNDRED-PLUS MOST COMMON VA SECONDARY CLAIMS

I could probably sell this guide for $97 or more (it's worth it), but for a limited time, you can download the ebook version right here, right now, at no cost. Here's a sliver of what you'll learn:

- Part 1: The five types of service connection explained from A to Z—simple answers make it clear exactly why secondary service connection might be key for you (even if you don't know where to start).
- Part 2: The definitive list of the top VA secondary claims for secondary service connection of more than one hundred conditions listed in detail—you'll learn how to make a secondary claim. Plus, we've included medical research studies and BVA examples for each condition. It's two hundred pages of solid gold, with clickable links!
- Part 3: BONUS RESOURCES! Grab your free bonuses today, including digital downloads and step-by-step video tutorials, to learn how to increase your VA disability rating faster— even if you've already filed or been denied.

Scan this QR code now to secure your instant free digital download of "Secondary Service Connection SECRETS!"

FOURTEEN-DAY ALL-ACCESS MEMBERSHIP

Having trouble understanding your Department of Defense and VA disability rating schedule? Frustrated by the bureaucracy of the military disability system? We understand. This incredible web resource has simplified, categorized, and indexed the entire VA schedule for rating disabilities. Whether you want a general overview of the 834 medical conditions that can be service connected and compensated under the law or you want to search for a very specific part of the law regarding one component of your claim, this is your resource.

The site breaks down each condition by name and medical lingo, and it includes pictures. Say you've had surgery on your left shoulder and can move it up to only a 45-degree angle. This website will tell you exactly what the rating should be for your level of disability.

This resource is also a way for us to be of service to the active-duty community. If you're on active duty and being medboarded, we can help you understand what's happening and how to get the outcome you deserve. This site is the world's most comprehensive and intuitive resource for navigating the entire VA disability rating system. Don't get frustrated—get rated! Visit MilitaryDisabilityMadeEasy.com or scan this QR code now to start your fourteen-day free trial of Military Disability Made Easy:

SEARCHABLE SITES

Next, I'm going to share some of the websites I visit almost every day to help veterans like you. These comprehensive sites allow you to quickly get answers to the trickiest claims questions.

GOOGLE

Type the topic keywords; search; find; read; interpret; apply; build on; create; explain the why, how, and what; and write it down.

VETNEXT AI

The world's number-one AI chatbot for VA disability claims. It provides fast, accurate answers for veterans navigating the complex VA claim process. Simply type your question and watch VetNext AI give you an insanely awesome answer.

CHATGPT

ChatGPT is an advanced language model developed by OpenAI based on the Generative Pre-trained Transformer (GPT) architecture. It's designed to understand and generate humanlike text based on the input it receives, making it capable of conversing, answering questions, and providing information or suggestions across a wide range of topics. It is epic for fast and free VA disability–related knowledge. Note: ChatGPT can make mistakes. Consider fact-checking important information.

M21-1 ADJUDICATION PROCEDURES MANUAL

This is what VA raters use to review and rate VA claims. It's a compilation of laws, regulations, and VA policies and procedures. Type the topic keywords; search; find; read; interpret; apply; build on; create; explain the why, how, and what; and write it down.

38 CFR BOOK C, PART 4, SCHEDULE FOR RATING DISABILITIES

This is the regulation that governs all VA disability conditions. Take the time to study it. Learn to search by keyword. For example, once you open the link, you can hit "CTRL+F" on your keyboard and search the lengthy law by keyword. You'll find the names of all ratable VA disability conditions by their medical terminology, including specific symptoms that warrant certain VA ratings under the law.

MILITARY DISABILITY MADE EASY

This website is 38 CFR Book C, Part 4, "Schedule for Rating Disabilities" on STEROIDS. You can start your free fourteen-day trial on the website. You can search and find by keyword, including pictures, more-detailed "Made-Easy" answers, etc. It's a GAME CHANGER.

ACKNOWLEDGMENTS

THANK YOU TO MY LORD AND SAVIOR, JESUS CHRIST, WHO died on the cross for my sins. You are the way and the truth and the life. I put my faith and life in your hands.

Many thanks to my wife, Laurel Reese, who is my partner and best friend. You're the calm to my storm. Your constant encouragement, patience, and insights made our movement and this book possible. I love you with all my heart.

Thanks to my three incredible children, Dylan, Everley, and Remington Reese, for your fun, your laughter, and the continued blessings you bring to my life. You're my world. I love you so much.

A big "thank you" to the editing and book-launch team of Rob Nichols and Thirdy Rivera. This incredible gift of VA claim knowledge for veterans would not have been possible without your countless hours researching, writing, and editing.

ABOUT THE AUTHOR

BRIAN REESE is one of the top VA disability benefits experts in the world and the number-one Amazon bestselling author of *You Deserve It: The Definitive Guide to Getting the Veteran Benefits You've Earned.*

Brian's frustration with the VA claim process led him to create VA Claims Insider, which provides disabled veterans with tips, strategies, and lessons learned to win their VA disability compensation claim faster, even if they've already filed, been denied, given up, or don't know where to start.

As the founder of VA Claims Insider and CEO of Military Disability Made Easy, Brian has helped serve more than ten million military members and veterans since 2013 through free online educational resources.

Brian is a former active-duty US Air Force officer with extensive experience leading hundreds of individuals and multifunctional teams in challenging international environments, including a combat tour to Afghanistan in 2011 supporting Operation ENDURING FREEDOM.

Brian is a Distinguished Graduate of Management from the

United States Air Force Academy, Colorado Springs, Colorado, and he holds an MBA from Oklahoma State University's Spears School of Business in Stillwater, Oklahoma, where he was a National Honor Scholar (top 1 percent of his graduate school class).

Made in United States
North Haven, CT
27 March 2025

67286985R00109